JAMESTOWN EDUCATION

Reading in the Content Areas

MATHEMATICS

Based on the work of Walter Pauk

Mc Graw Hill Glencoe

New York, New York   Columbus, Ohio   Chicago, Illinois   Peoria, Illinois   Woodland Hills, California

JAMESTOWN EDUCATION

Readability

Tab 1: Levels D–F
Tab 2: Levels G–I
Tab 3: Levels J–K
Tab 4: Levels L–L+

Cover photo: © Tom Sanders/CORBIS

Glencoe

The McGraw-Hill Companies

ISBN: 0-07-861706-5

Send all queries to:
Glencoe/McGraw-Hill
8787 Orion Place
Columbus, OH 43240-4027

5 6 7 8 9 10 079 10 09 08 07 06

Contents

To the Student

To succeed in the courses you take, one of the most important skills you can have is good reading ability. Different courses require different types of reading. If material is easy for you or you have studied it before, you may read quickly. If the material is new or difficult, you may read slowly. In fact, you may read the material several times. You can use the reading skills featured in this book in all your courses.

The passages in the book are readings in mathematics. Within this subject area are several subcategories, including geometry, finance, and math puzzles.

This book does not require you to master many new facts. Instead, its purpose is to show you *how to read math-related information*. You will learn techniques that textbook writers use to organize material. You will see how new information can be added to what you already know. And you will learn about the six skills that can help you read just about anything.

The Six Types of Questions

In this book, the basic skills necessary for reading factual material are taught through the use of the following six types of questions: main idea, subject matter, supporting details, conclusion, clarifying devices, and vocabulary in context.

Main Idea. Whenever you read, ask yourself, What point is the writer trying to make? If you look for an answer to this question, you will probably find one. But if you don't focus, all things may seem equal. Nothing will stand out.

Try to find the main idea in the following passage by asking yourself, What point is the writer trying to make?

> The abacus is an instrument that helps keep track of calculations. A frame holds wooden beads that are moved as they are counted. Beads in the far-right column are "ones." Beads in the columns to the left are tens, hundreds, and so on. The abacus has been used for nearly a thousand years in China. It is still used today in Asia, especially by elderly shopkeepers. Many say they can work faster with an abacus than with a computer.

What is the main idea? Here is a good answer: The abacus is an instrument that helps keep track of calculations. This passage is fairly easy to figure out because the first sentence is an excellent topic sentence.

The next example does not have a topic sentence. Nevertheless, you can still answer the question, What point is the writer trying to make? This time, think about the passage and come up with your own answer.

The figure at the right is a parallelogram. You can be sure that a figure is a parallelogram if both pairs of opposite sides are parallel or if both pairs of opposite sides are the same length. For another way to tell that a figure is a parallelogram, look at one pair of opposite sides. If those two sides are parallel and equal in length, then the figure is a parallelogram.

This passage may have required a bit more thought because the correct answer is a summary-type answer. Compare your answer with the following main idea statement: There are many ways to tell that a figure is a parallelogram.

Subject Matter. This question looks easy and often is easy. But don't let that fool you into thinking it isn't important. The subject matter question can help you with the most important skill of all in reading and learning: concentration. With it, you comprehend and learn. Without it, you fail.

Here is the secret for concentrating: After reading a few lines of a passage, ask yourself, What is the subject matter of this passage? Instantly you will be thinking about the passage. You will be concentrating. If you don't ask this question, your eyes will move across the lines of print, yet your mind may be thinking of other things.

By asking this question as you read each passage in this book, you will master the skill so well that it will carry over to everything you read.

Let's see how this method works. Here is a short passage.

Architecture students work together to build models for their buildings. Some students cut accurately scaled shapes for the walls, floors, and roofs. Other students glue the shapes together, so sections of the building can be lifted away to reveal the inner rooms. Still others create trees, cars, and people that can be placed alongside the model building.

On finishing the first sentence, your thought should have been something like this: *Ah, a passage on models. Maybe I can learn how they are made.* If it was, your head was in the right place. By focusing right away on the subject matter, you will be concentrating, you will be looking for something, your attitude will be superb, and—best of all—you will be understanding, learning, and remembering.

Supporting Details. In common usage, the word *detail* has taken on the meaning of "something relatively unimportant." But details are important. Details are the plaster, board, and brick of a building, while main ideas are the large strong steel or wooden beams. A solid, well-written passage must contain both.

The bulk of a factual passage is made up of details that support the main idea. The main idea is often buried among the details. You have to dig to distinguish between the main idea and the details. Here are some characteristics that can help you see the difference between supporting details and main ideas.

First, supporting details come in various forms. They can be examples, explanations, descriptions, definitions, comparisons, contrasts, exceptions, analogies, similes, and metaphors.

Second, these various kinds of details are used to support the main idea. The words themselves—*supporting details*—spell out their job. When you have trouble finding the main idea, take a passage apart sentence by sentence. Asking yourself, Does this sentence support something, or is this the idea being supported? You must not only separate the main idea from the details, you must also see how they help one another. The main idea can often be expressed in a sentence. But a sentence cannot tell a complete story. The writer must use additional sentences to give a full picture.

The following passage shows how important details are for providing a full picture of what the writer had in mind.

> The mathematical equation $a + b \times a - b = a^2 - b^2$ is a simple but powerful tool. In arithmetic, it lets you calculate 51×49 in your head.
>
> $$(50 + 1)(50 - 1) = 50^2 - 1^2 = 2{,}500 - 1 = 2{,}499$$
>
> In algebra, it lets you factor $16x^2 - 25y^2$ as $(4x + 5y)(4x - 5y)$.

Here the main idea is in the first sentence. Having stated the main idea, the writer goes on to give example after example showing why it is true. The examples are supporting details.

Conclusion. As a reader moves through a passage, grasping the main idea and the supporting details, it is natural for him or her to begin to guess an ending or a conclusion. Some passages contain conclusions; others do not. It all depends on the writer's purpose. For example, some passages simply describe a process—how something is done. It is not always necessary to draw a conclusion from such a passage.

In some passages with conclusions, the writer states the conclusion. But in most passages in this book, the conclusion is merely implied. That is, the writer seems to have come to a conclusion but has not stated it. You must draw that conclusion.

In the following passage, the author implies a conclusion but does not state it.

> The Iditarod is an annual sled dog race run to commemorate a race against time. In 1925, when diphtheria vaccine was needed in Nome, Alaska, a dog sled was the only means of delivering the medicine. The Iditarod is run in about 25 stages. The 2003 winner, Robert Sorlie, covered the 52 miles from Ruby to Galena in 6 hours and 29 minutes. Then he traveled the 52 miles from Galena to Nulato in 10 hours and 46 minutes. When Sorlie and his dogs crossed the finish line, they had run 1,121 miles in 9 days, 15 hours, 47 minutes, and 36 seconds.

From this passage, we can draw the conclusion that the sleds travel at very different speeds along the various stages of this difficult trail.

Sometimes a writer will ask you to draw a conclusion by applying what you have learned to a new situation, as in the following passage.

> Ben Franklin helped write the U.S. Constitution, experimented with electricity, organized a fire department, and invented bifocals. But that was not enough. In his will, he said, "I wish to be useful even after my Death." Franklin gave the city of Philadelphia about $4,000 and a plan for lending the money so that the sum would grow. After 100 years, Philadelphia had about $172,000. The city used some of that money to finance a science museum and reinvested about $40,000. After the second 100 years, that $40,000 had grown to $2\frac{1}{4}$ million dollars!

If you were asked what this passage suggests about investing money, you would have to generalize beyond the passage. You might draw the conclusion that when you invest money, you cannot predict how much your investment will grow.

Looking for a conclusion puts you in the shoes of a detective. You must think, *Where is the writer going? What conclusion can I draw?* And, like a detective, you must try to guess the conclusion, changing the guess as you get more information.

Clarifying Devices. Clarifying devices are words, phrases, and techniques that a writer uses to make main ideas and supporting details clear and interesting. By knowing some of these clarifying and controlling devices, you will be better able to recognize them in the passages you read. By recognizing them, you will be able to read with greater comprehension and speed.

Transitional or Signal Words. The largest single group of clarifying devices, and the most widely used, is transitional or signal words. Here are some signal words that you see all the time: *first, second, next, last,* and *finally.* A writer uses such words to keep ideas, steps in a process, or lists in order. Other transitional words include *however, in brief, in conclusion, above all, therefore, since, because,* and *consequently.*

When you see transitional words, consider what they mean. A transitional word like *or* tells you that another option, or choice, is coming. Words like *but* and *however* signal that a contrast, or change in point of view, will follow.

Organizational Patterns. Organizational patterns are also clarifying devices. One such pattern is the chronological pattern, in which events unfold in the order of time: one thing happens first, then another, and so on. A time pattern orders events. The incident may take place in five minutes or over a period of hundreds of years.

There are other organizational patterns as well. Writers use spatial descriptions to tell how things look. They list examples. In science writing, they use scientific data. Seeing the organizational pattern will help you read the material.

Textual Devices. Textbook writers often use patterns or particular text styles to make their ideas clear. Bulleted lists, subheads, and boldfaced or italicized words help to highlight important ideas in the text. Concepts shown in charts or diagrams may be easier to understand than concepts explained in words alone.

Literal Versus Figurative Language. Sometimes words do not mean what they seem to mean on first reading. For example, a writer may say, "The tragedy shattered the hero of the story." You may know *shattered* means "breaking into pieces." The word is often applied to breakable objects, but here it is applied to a person's feelings. Being alert to special meanings can help you appreciate the writer's meaning.

Two literary devices that writers use to present ideas in interesting ways are similes (SIM-a-leez) and metaphors (MET-a-forz). Both are used to make comparisons that add color and power to ideas. A simile uses the word *like* or *as.* Here's an example of a simile: She has a mind like a computer. Here, a person's mind is compared to a computer. A metaphor makes a direct comparison: Her mind is a computer.

Vocabulary in Context. How accurate are you in using words you think you already know? Do you know that the word *exotic* means "a thing or a person from a foreign country"? Exotic flowers and exotic costumes are flowers and costumes from foreign countries. *Exotic* has been used incorrectly so often and for so long that it has developed a second meaning. Many people use *exotic* to mean "strikingly unusual, as in color or design."

Many people think that the words *imply* and *infer* mean the same thing. They do not. A writer may imply, or suggest, something. The reader then infers what the writer implied. In other words, to imply is to "suggest an idea." To infer is to "take meaning out" or to "draw a conclusion."

It is easy to see what would happen to a passage if a reader skipped a word or two that he or she did not know and imposed fuzzy meanings on a few others. The result would inevitably be a gross misunderstanding of the writer's message. You will become a better reader if you learn the exact meanings and the various shades of meaning of the words that are already familiar to you.

In this book, you should be able to figure out the meanings of many words from their context—that is, from the words and phrases around them. If this method does not work for you, however, you may consult a dictionary.

Answering the Main Idea Question

The main idea questions in this book are not the usual multiple-choice variety that asks you to select the one correct statement. Rather, you are given three statements and are asked to select the statement that expresses the main idea of the passage, the statement that is too narrow, and the statement that is too broad. You have to work hard to identify all three statements correctly. This new type of question teaches you to recognize the differences between statements that, at first, seem almost equal.

To help you handle these questions, let's go behind the scenes to see how the main idea questions in this book were constructed. The true main idea statement was always written first. It had to be neat and succinct. The main idea tells who or what is the subject of the passage. The main idea statement also tells what the subject is doing or what the subject is like. Next, keeping the main idea statement in mind, the other two statements were written. They are variations of the main idea statement. The "too narrow" statement had to express only part of the main idea. The "too broad" statement had to be very general in scope.

Read the passage below. Then, to learn how to answer the main idea questions, follow the instructions in the box. The answer to each part of the question has been filled in for you. The score for each answer has also been marked.

The Long and Short of It

Every day we lace our talk with measurement words. We ask, "How much?" "How many?" and "How far?" At the store, we buy meat by the pound and cloth by the yard. All athletic events are played on measured fields or surfaces. In football, for example, we know that a first down means a gain of at least 10 yards. Words of distance, weight, and size help us understand and visualize what is seen or said.

In ancient times, people used parts of the body as units of measurement. The Romans used *uncia* to name the distance equal to the width of a thumb. The English picked up this word and changed it to *inch*. However, rather than use the thumb as a unit, they decided that an inch should be "three barley corns, round and dry, placed end-to-end lengthwise."

After the inch measurement was accepted, the English joined 12 inches and called that length a *foot*. As it happened, 12 inches was roughly the length of a person's foot, so the foot-unit was widely used.

Then the English introduced a larger unit, the *yard*. Three foot lengths make a yard. A yard is also roughly the distance from the nose to the tip of an outstretched hand.

Of course, there is a flaw in all this. Not all people are the same size. But no one seemed to care.

	Answer	Score
Mark the *main idea*	M	15
Mark the statement that is *too broad*	B	5
Mark the statement that is *too narrow*	N	5

a. Various units of measurement
developed over the centuries.   M   15

[This statement gathers all the important
points. It gives a correct picture of the
main idea in a brief way: (1) various
units, (2) used for measuring,
(3) developed over time.]

b. The problems of measurement
began centuries ago.   N   5

[This statement is too broad. It refers to
measurement and ancient times, but it
doesn't tell about the specific ideas in the
passage.]

c. The English recognized the need for
a standard inch.   B   5

[This statement is correct, but it is too
narrow. It refers to only one of the measurement units discussed in the passage.]

Getting the Most Out of This Book

The following steps could be called "tricks of the trade" or "rules for learning." It
doesn't matter what they are called. What does matter is that they work.

Think about the title. A famous language expert proposes the following "trick" to
use when reading. "The first thing to do is to read the title. Then spend a few
moments thinking about it."

Writers spend time thinking up good titles. They pack a lot of meaning into
titles. It makes sense for you to spend a few seconds trying to dig out some meaning. These moments of thought will give you a head start on a passage.

Thinking about the title can help you in another way too. It helps you concen-
trate on a passage before you begin reading. Why does this happen? Thinking about
the title fills your head with thoughts about the passage. There's no room for anything else to get in to break your concentration.

The Dot Step. Here is a method that will speed up your reading. It also builds comprehension at the same time.

Spend a few moments with the title. Then read quickly through the passage. Next, without looking back, answer the six questions by placing a dot in the box next to each answer of your choice. The dots will be your "unofficial" answers. For the main idea question (question 1), place your dot in the box next to the statement that you think is the main idea.

The dot system helps you think hard on your first fast reading. The practice you gain by trying to grasp and remember ideas makes you a stronger reader.

The Checkmark Step. First, answer the main idea question. Follow the steps that are given above each set of statements for this question. Use a capital letter to mark your final answer to each part of the main idea question.

You have answered the other five questions with a dot. Now read the passage once more carefully. This time, mark your final answer to each question by placing a checkmark (√) in the box next to the answer of your choice. The answers with the checkmarks are the ones that will count toward your score.

The Diagnostic Chart. Now move your final answers to the Diagnostic Chart for the passage. These charts start on page 155.

Use the row of boxes beside Passage 1 for the answers to the first passage. Use the row of boxes beside Passage 2 for the answers to the second passage, and so on. Write the letter of your answer to the left of the dotted line in each block.

Correct your answers using the Answer Keys on pages 152–154. When scoring your answers, do not use an *x* for incorrect or a *c* for correct. Instead, use this method: If your choice is incorrect, write the letter of the correct answer to the right of the dotted line in the block.

Thus, the row of answers for each passage will show your incorrect answers. And it will also show the correct answers.

Your Total Comprehension Score. Go back to the passage you have just read. If you answered a question incorrectly, draw a line under the correct choice on the question page. Then write your score for each question on the line provided. Add the scores to get your total comprehension score. Enter that number in the box marked Total Score.

Graphing Your Progress. After you have found your total comprehension score, turn to the Progress Graphs that begin on page 158. Write your score in the box under the number of the passage. Then put an *x* along the line above the box to show your total comprehension score. Join the *x*'s as you go. This will plot a line showing your progress.

Taking Corrective Action. Your incorrect answers give you a way to teach yourself how to read better. Take the time to study these answers.

Go back to the questions. For each question you answered wrong, read the correct answer (the one you have underlined) several times. With the correct answer in mind, go back to the passage itself. Read to see why the given answer is better. Try to see where you made your mistake and why you chose an incorrect answer.

The Steps in a Nutshell

Here's a quick review of the steps to follow. Following these steps is the way to get the most out of this book. Be sure you have read and understood everything in this To the Student section before you begin reading the passage.

1. **Think about the title of the passage.** Try to get all the meaning the writer put into it.
2. **Read the passage quickly.**
3. **Answer the questions, using the dot system.** Use dots to mark your unofficial answers. Don't look back at the passage.
4. **Read the passage again—carefully.**
5. **Mark your final answers.** Put a checkmark (√) in the box to note your final answer. Use capital letters for each part of the main idea question.
6. **Mark your answers on the diagnostic chart.** Record your final answers on the diagnostic chart for the passage. Write your answers to the left of the dotted line in the answer blocks for the passage.
7. **Correct your answers.** Use the answer keys on pages 152–154. If an answer is not correct, write the correct answer on the right side of the block, beside your incorrect answer. Then go back to the question page. Place a line under the correct answer.
8. **Find your total comprehension score.** Find this by adding up the points you earned for each question. Enter the total in the box marked Total Score.
9. **Graph your progress.** Enter and plot your score on the progress graph for that passage.
10. **Take corrective action.** Read your wrong answers. Read the passage once more. Try to figure out why you were wrong.

To the Teacher

The Reading Passages

Each of the 75 passages included in the book is related to mathematics. Within this subject area are several subcategories, for example, geometry, finance, and math puzzles.

Each passage had to meet the following two criteria: high interest level and appropriate readability level. The high interest level was assured by choosing passages of mature content that would appeal to a wide range of readers.

The readability level of each passage was computed by applying Dr. Edward B. Fry's *Formula for Estimating Readability.* The passages are arranged within the book according to reading levels. *Reading in the Content Areas: Mathematics* contains 75 passages that range from reading level 4 to reading level 12+. The passages are organized into four ranges of reading levels, as indicated by color tabs: The first passages range from reading level 4 to reading level 6. The next passages range from reading level 7 to reading level 9. The third group of passages ranges from reading level 10 to reading level 11. The final passages range from reading level 12 to reading level 12+.

The Six Questions

This book is organized around six essential questions. The most important of these is the main idea question, which is actually a set of three statements. Students must first choose and label the statement that expresses the main idea of the passage; then they must label each of the other statements as either too narrow or too broad to be the main idea.

In addition to the main idea question, there are five other questions. These questions are within the framework of the following five categories: subject matter, supporting details, conclusion, clarifying devices, and vocabulary in context.

By repeated practice with answering the questions within these six categories, students will develop an active searching attitude about what they read. These six types of questions will help them become aware of what they are reading at the time they are actually seeing the words and phrases on a page. This thinking-while-reading sets the stage for higher comprehension and better retention.

The Diagnostic Chart

The Diagnostic Chart provides the most dignified form of guidance yet devised. With this chart, no one has to point out a student's weaknesses. The chart does that automatically, yielding the information directly and personally to the student, making self-teaching possible. The organization of the questions and the format for marking answers on the chart are what make it work so well.

The six questions for each passage are always in the same order. For example, the question designed to teach the skill of drawing conclusions is always the fourth question, and the main idea question is always first. Keeping the questions in order sets the stage for the smooth working of the chart.

The chart works automatically when students write the letter of their answer choices for each passage in the spaces provided. Even after completing only one passage, the chart will reveal the types of questions answered correctly as well as the types answered incorrectly. As the answers for more passages are recorded, the chart will show the types of questions that are missed consistently. A pattern can be seen after three or more passages have been completed. For example, if a student answers question 4 (drawing conclusions) incorrectly for three out of four passages, the student's weakness in this area shows up automatically.

Once a weakness is revealed, have your students take the following steps: First, turn to the instructional pages in the beginning of the book and study the section in which the topic is discussed. Second, go back and reread the questions that were missed in that particular category. Then, with the correct answer to a question in mind, read the entire passage again, trying to see how the writer developed the answer to the question. Do this for each question that was missed. Third, when reading future passages, make an extra effort to correctly answer the questions in that particular category. Fourth, if the difficulty continues, arrange to see your teacher.

Reading in the Content Areas
MATHEMATICS

1 Getting Help with Math

It's nine o'clock on a Tuesday night. You are trying to finish your math assignment. You have only two problems left to go. Almost done! You are looking forward to a nice snack and your favorite TV show. You read the next problem and groan. You don't have a clue how to do it. You may check your notes from class. Or you may try reading your textbook. But the problem might as well be written in a foreign language.

Does this sound familiar? Most people who have taken any kind of math class have had this experience. What do you do when you get stuck? Perhaps you call a friend. Or you ask a family member for help. But what if it's late at night?

Years ago there were very few ways to get help if you were stuck on a math problem. Math is different from other school subjects. You often cannot find what to do in a book. A dictionary or even an encyclopedia probably won't help you. You need someone to show you the steps. Learning most kinds of math is something like learning to play a musical instrument. You need a <u>coach</u> to show you what to do.

In many areas there are homework telephone lines. These hot lines have volunteers. They can help you do homework in all subjects. A math volunteer can explain the steps in a math problem that has you stumped.

Today you can also get help on the Internet. There are several homework help programs and Web pages. In some, you leave your question on a message board. Or you write it in an e-mail note. In other math-help programs there are live volunteer teachers. You can wait for a real math teacher to help you do the problem.

Main Idea 1		Answer	Score
Mark the *main idea*		**M**	15
Mark the statement that is *too broad*		**B**	5
Mark the statement that is *too narrow*		**N**	5

a. Dictionaries and encyclopedias won't help you do math homework. ☐ _____

b. There are various ways to get help if you have trouble with math homework. ☐ _____

c. A lot of students find it hard to do math. ☐ _____

Score 15 points for each correct answer.   **Score**

Subject Matter   **2**   This passage is mostly concerned with
       ☐ a. why math is difficult to do.
       ☐ b. ways of getting help with math homework.
       ☐ c. using reference books to do math homework.
       ☐ d. using a computer to do math.   _____

Supporting   **3**   In the first paragraph, the writer asks you to
Details   ☐ a. solve a math problem.
       ☐ b. recall how you once asked someone to
           help you with math.
       ☐ c. use a computer to get help in math homework.
       ☐ d. imagine yourself doing math homework.   _____

Conclusion   **4**   The passage suggests that people who need math
homework help should
       ☐ a. not take any more math classes.
       ☐ b. try a homework help program on the Internet.
       ☐ c. watch some television.
       ☐ d. write an e-mail note to a friend.   _____

Clarifying   **5**   The writer compares learning math to
Devices   ☐ a. learning to play a musical instrument.
       ☐ b. using a computer.
       ☐ c. finishing a homework assignment.
       ☐ d. calling a friend to get help on homework.   _____

Vocabulary   **6**   In this passage, the word <u>coach</u> means
in Context   ☐ a. someone who teaches a sport.
       ☐ b. someone who can explain math problems.
       ☐ c. someone who will solve problems for you.
       ☐ d. the head of an Internet Web site.   _____

Add your scores for questions 1–6. Enter the total here   **Total**
and on the graph on page 158.   **Score**   _____

2 Visualizing Percentages

Many people find percentages difficult. A percentage is different from a number such as 25. You can imagine 25 golf balls. Or you might think of 25 dollars or 25 feet. Twenty-five of something is easy to visualize. You can picture it in your mind.

It is harder to form a mental picture of 25 percent. A percentage compares things. It compares the number to 100. Think of the percent sign (%) as meaning "out of 100." Thus 25 percent means "25 out of 100." This may help you understand what 25 percent means. But it doesn't help you make a mental picture of 25 percent.

To picture 25 percent, you need an example. That is because 25 percent can mean different things. Getting 25 percent of a small number is different from getting 25 percent of a large number. For example, 25 percent of $83 is much less than 25 percent of $8,300.

Is there a way to picture an example like 25 percent of $83? One way is to sketch two bars, both of the same length. One bar, the percent bar, has 100 units. The other, the number bar, has 83 units.

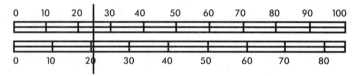

Notice that the sketch has a <u>vertical</u> line. This line goes through 25 on the percent bar and hits the number bar at about 21. So the diagram helps you "see" a percentage. It shows that 25 percent of $83 is about $21.

Making bar diagrams for percentages can assist you in comprehending what the percentages mean. Your diagrams need not be beautiful; in fact, they can be rough. They are also a useful way to doublecheck answers you arrive at with a calculator.

Main Idea   1

	Answer	Score
Mark the *main idea*	**M**	15
Mark the statement that is *too broad*	**B**	5
Mark the statement that is *too narrow*	**N**	5

a. A bar diagram can help you if you have trouble picturing percentages. ☐ _____

b. Solving problems with percentages is a useful skill. ☐ _____

c. Twenty-five percent of 83 is about 21. ☐ _____

Score 15 points for each correct answer.   Score

Subject Matter   2   This passage is mainly about
    ☐ a. doing percentage problems in your head.
    ☐ b. using a calculator for percentage problems.
    ☐ c. estimating percentages with diagrams.
    ☐ d. finding percentages of large numbers.   _____

Supporting Details   3   If you draw a percent diagram, the two bars in it must be
    ☐ a. four inches long.
    ☐ b. divided into 10 equal parts.
    ☐ c. drawn on graph paper.
    ☐ d. the same length.   _____

Conclusion   4   The first three paragraphs explain why
    ☐ a. percentages are not numbers.
    ☐ b. it is difficult to make mental pictures of percentages.
    ☐ c. 25 percent of $83 is about $21.
    ☐ d. 25 golf balls is different from 25 dollars.   _____

Clarifying Devices   5   A percentage diagram would **not** help you
    ☐ a. to estimate an answer to a percentage problem.
    ☐ b. to check an answer to a percentage problem.
    ☐ c. to avoid errors in percentage problems.
    ☐ d. if you didn't know what *percent* means.   _____

Vocabulary in Context   6   The word <u>vertical</u> means
    ☐ a. from side to side.
    ☐ b. diagonal.
    ☐ c. up and down.
    ☐ d. made up of several small pieces.   _____

Add your scores for questions 1–6. Enter the total here and on the graph on page 158.   Total Score   _____

5

3 Are We There Yet?

If you are like most people, you have probably been lost on a car trip. You may stop and ask directions, but sometimes the directions aren't helpful. Sometimes they may even be wrong! The best way to not get lost is to learn to use road maps.

The first thing to understand about road maps is the scale. The scale on a map tells you how the map relates to the actual area it is showing. For example, you may see a note on a map saying "1 in. = 150 miles." On this map, each inch stands for 150 miles. A distance of 10 inches equals 1,500 miles ($10 \times 150 = 1,500$). If the map is 20 inches wide, it could show the whole United States.

A map with the scale 1 in. = 150 miles can help you plan a car trip from Boston to Los Angeles, but it will not help you find your way around city streets. For this you need a city street map. The scale on this map will be different. For instance, every inch may show one half of a mile. A map isn't useful if it doesn't have the right scale for your trip.

The second tip for using road maps is finding two locations. You need to know where you are right now and where you want to go. Then select the roads or streets you will use to get there. Use the <u>intersections</u> of large streets or highways to help you zero in on locations.

Finally, it is an excellent idea to keep a small compass in your car. The compass will tell you if you are driving north, south, or some other direction. On most road maps, north is at the top. Turn the map so the top edge is towards north. This can help you avoid driving in the opposite direction.

It may take some practice to learn to use road maps. But if you have a map with the right scale and know how to use it, you will never get lost again.

Main Idea	1		
		Answer	**Score**
Mark the *main idea*		M	15
Mark the statement that is *too broad*		B	5
Mark the statement that is *too narrow*		N	5

a. A map scale shows how distances on the map are related to real distances. ☐ _____

b. Road maps give useful information. ☐ _____

c. Using a road map will help you not get lost on a car trip. ☐ _____

Score 15 points for each correct answer.   Score

Subject Matter   **2**   Another good title for this passage would be
      □ a. Finding the Distance Between Two Cities.
      □ b. Learning to Use Road Maps.
      □ c. Understanding How a Compass Works.
      □ d. Estimating Costs for a Car Trip.   _____

Supporting   **3**   On a map with a scale of 1 in. = 150 miles,
Details   10 inches represents
      □ a. 15 miles.
      □ b. 150 miles.
      □ c. 1,500 miles.
      □ d. 15,000 miles.   _____

Conclusion   **4**   A road map won't help you on a trip if you
      □ a. don't know where you are to begin with.
      □ b. don't have a compass.
      □ c. turn the map so the top edge is north.
      □ d. don't know the distance between two locations.   _____

Clarifying   **5**   The writer explains the idea of a map scale by
Devices   □ a. describing a diagram.
      □ b. giving tips for using a map.
      □ c. giving an example.
      □ d. telling a story in which people got lost.   _____

Vocabulary   **6**   In this passage, the word <u>intersections</u> means
in Context   □ a. places where two streets meet.
      □ b. two cars crashing into each other.
      □ c. lines to help you fold a street map.
      □ d. ways to cut maps into smaller sections.   _____

Add your scores for questions 1–6. Enter the total here   **Total**
and on the graph on page 158.   **Score**   _____

4 The Tangram Puzzle

Tangrams are old puzzles. They have been found in Chinese books hundreds of years old. During the 1800s, tangrams were very popular in both Europe and the United States. And the puzzles are still enjoyed today.

The tangram puzzle is easy to describe. There are seven geometric pieces. Five pieces are right triangles. There are two large triangles, one medium triangle, and two small triangles. There are two other pieces, a square and a 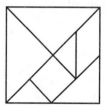 parallelogram. You move the pieces around to make different shapes. For example, the pieces can make a large square. The tangram square is shown in the diagram at the right.

A book of tangram puzzles shows black outlines of shapes. The challenge is to use all the pieces to make one of the black outlines. There are many geometric shapes to make. Some of the puzzles look like animals and birds. You can also make letters and human figures.

You can buy tangram puzzle pieces made of plastic or wood. But it is easy to make your own set. Draw the pieces on graph paper. Follow the heavy lines in the diagram. Cut the shapes apart. You will have your own set of tangram pieces. As your first puzzle, put the square back together. Next, try making one large triangle. Remember to use all seven pieces. Then try a rectangle.

Perhaps you'll find you like working with tangrams. There are many puzzle books using these shapes. Warning: Playing with the pieces can become addictive!

Main Idea	1			
			Answer	Score
	Mark the *main idea*		M	15
	Mark the statement that is *too broad*		B	5
	Mark the statement that is *too narrow*		N	5

a. The seven tangram pieces can make a square. ☐ _____

b. The tangram puzzle is made from seven geometric shapes. ☐ _____

c. People throughout the ages have liked doing puzzles. ☐ _____

Score 15 points for each correct answer. Score

Subject Matter   **2**   This passage is mostly concerned with
☐ a. describing how the tangram puzzle works.
☐ b. giving hints for solving tangram puzzles.
☐ c. the history of puzzles.
☐ d. defining figures like squares and triangles. _____

Supporting   **3**   How many of the tangram pieces are **not**
Details   triangles?
☐ a. 0
☐ b. 1
☐ c. 2
☐ d. 7 _____

Conclusion   **4**   From the last paragraph, you can conclude that
tangram puzzles are
☐ a. difficult.
☐ b. easy.
☐ c. only for children.
☐ d. fun for many people. _____

Clarifying   **5**   To make a set of tangram puzzle pieces, you
Devices   need only to
☐ a. know the geometric names of the pieces.
☐ b. copy the diagram.
☐ c. understand geometry.
☐ d. use the pieces to make an animal or bird. _____

Vocabulary   **6**   In this passage, the word <u>parallelogram</u> means
in Context
☐ a. a three-sided shape.
☐ b. a four-sided shape that is not a square.
☐ c. a five-sided shape.
☐ d. an oval shape. _____

Add your scores for questions 1–6. Enter the total here   **Total**
and on the graph on page 158.   **Score** _____

5 Calculators and Repeating Decimals

Calculators are great tools. They help you do math quickly. They show exact answers to difficult problems. Are calculators always right? It depends on what you mean by right. You may be adding, subtracting, or multiplying. Then a calculator will show the exact answer. But dividing is different. Try dividing 10 by 6 on a calculator. You may get 1.6666666. Or you may get 1.6666667. Which is the exact answer, 1.6666666 or 1.6666667? Neither! Both are approximations. They are both right. But neither is exact.

Why do calculators do this? Most of them can't show fractions. The exact answer to 10 divided by 6 is the mixed number $1\frac{2}{3}$. The calculator has no way to display two-thirds.

$$
\begin{array}{r}
1.66\ldots \\
6\overline{)10.00\ldots} \\
\underline{-6} \\
40 \\
\underline{-36} \\
40 \\
\underline{-36} \\
4\ldots
\end{array}
$$

Here is a way to understand what is happening. Divide 10 by 6 using paper and pencil. Your problem will look like the one at the left. The answer has a repeating decimal. You can keep dividing forever. You'll never get an exact answer. The digit 6 in the answer repeats forever.

A calculator that gives 1.6666666 is truncating (cutting off) the answer. It shows as many digits as it can. Then it drops the rest. A calculator that gives 1.6666667 is rounding. Since the last digit is 5 or greater, it shows the next higher digit (7).

For most division problems, it won't matter if the answer is approximate. But you might have a problem in which you really need the exact answer. Then you may need to use fractions.

Main Idea 1

	Answer	Score
Mark the *main idea*	M	15
Mark the statement that is *too broad*	B	5
Mark the statement that is *too narrow*	N	5

a. Dividing 10 by 6 results in a repeating decimal. ☐ _____

b. Calculators are useful tools in math. ☐ _____

c. In division problems, calculators sometimes give approximate answers. ☐ _____

Score 15 points for each correct answer.   **Score**

Subject Matter   2   This passage is mainly about
- ☐ a. how to round off answers.
- ☐ b. multiplying with fractions.
- ☐ c. dividing numbers on a calculator.
- ☐ d. checking answers with a calculator.   _____

Supporting Details   3   A calculator answer of 1.6666667 is probably
- ☐ a. rounded.
- ☐ b. truncated.
- ☐ c. exact.
- ☐ d. not correct.   _____

Conclusion   4   What can you conclude from this passage?
- ☐ a. You should never divide numbers with a calculator.
- ☐ b. When you divide with a calculator, the answer may be approximate.
- ☐ c. All division problems have repeating decimals as answers.
- ☐ d. Exact answers are not important in division.   _____

Clarifying Devices   5   In the first paragraph, the writer shows the difference in meaning between right and
- ☐ a. wrong.
- ☐ b. exact.
- ☐ c. division.
- ☐ d. calculate.   _____

Vocabulary in Context   6   In this passage, the word <u>display</u> means
- ☐ a. draw a picture of.
- ☐ b. put into a store window.
- ☐ c. correct.
- ☐ d. show.   _____

Add your scores for questions 1–6. Enter the total here and on the graph on page 158.   **Total Score**   _____

6 Will Roman Numerals Return?

You've probably seen Roman numerals. But you haven't seen them very often. You can buy clocks and watches with Roman numerals. They use Roman numerals I (1) through XII (12) for the hours. The front pages in a book sometimes have Roman numerals for page numbers. Roman numerals can be also found on buildings. There they show the date the building was made. And some older movies and books use them. They show the copyright date.

The Roman system was developed by the ancient Romans. It uses the letters I, V, X, L, C, D, and M to stand for 1, 5, 10, 50, 100, 500, and 1000. Other numbers are made by combining the letters in different ways. The number 8 is VIII, formed by adding three ones to V. Sometimes subtraction is used. The numbers 4 and 9 are made this way. Four is five minus one, or IV. Nine is ten minus one, or IX. Notice that the part being subtracted comes first.

Roman numerals for dates can be very long. The year 1938 is written MCMXXXVIII. Dates in the 1800s are even longer. The date 1888 is written MDCCCLXXXVIII. Is isn't difficult to see why people stopped using Roman numerals for dates.

But numbers go in and out of <u>fashion</u>. Now that the 1900s have come to an end, Roman numerals may again have their turn. The year 2000 is a simple MM. The next ten years are pretty easy too. Here is how the list begins. First is MMI, then MMII, MMIII, MMIV, MMV.

The year 2000 was nicknamed Y2K. (K stands for 1000.) But 2000 could just as easily have been called MM. This is a shorter—and more tasty-sounding—abbreviation.

Main Idea	1	Answer	Score
	Mark the *main idea*	M	15
	Mark the statement that is *too broad*	B	5
	Mark the statement that is *too narrow*	N	5

a.	Roman numerals may be used more frequently in the future.	☐ ____
b.	Roman numerals use letters to stand for numbers.	☐ ____
c.	Dates can be written in many different ways.	☐ ____

Score 15 points for each correct answer.　　　　　　**Score**

Subject Matter　**2**　This passage is mostly concerned with
　　　☐ a. the meaning of Y2K.
　　　☐ b. telling time using Roman numerals.
　　　☐ c. how Roman numerals are written and used.
　　　☐ d. adding and subtracting Roman numerals.　　____

Supporting Details　**3**　The Roman numeral D stands for
　　　☐ a. 10.
　　　☐ b. 50.
　　　☐ c. 500.
　　　☐ d. 5000.　　____

Conclusion　**4**　The Roman numeral XL equals
　　　☐ a. 60 (10 is added to 50).
　　　☐ b. 11 (10 is added to 1).
　　　☐ c. 40 (10 is subtracted from 50).
　　　☐ d. 90 (10 is subtracted from 100).　　____

Clarifying Devices　**5**　The writer explains how Roman numerals are made by
　　　☐ a. showing diagrams.
　　　☐ b. relating them to clocks and watches.
　　　☐ c. proving mathematical statements.
　　　☐ d. giving examples.　　____

Vocabulary in Context　**6**　In this passage, the word <u>fashion</u> means
　　　☐ a. relating to clothing.
　　　☐ b. to create or make.
　　　☐ c. style or trend.
　　　☐ d. not in current use.　　____

Add your scores for questions 1–6. Enter the total here and on the graph on page 158.　　**Total Score**　____

7 The Digits of Pi

You may have a calculator with a pi key. This key shows the symbol π, which is a letter from the Greek alphabet. Why is π on one of the calculator keys?

Pi is a number that shows how parts of a circle relate to each other. To understand pi, imagine a circle. Now imagine a line that cuts the circle in half. This line is the diameter. To find a value for pi, use a soup can. The top or bottom of the can is a circle. Put a string around the circular part and measure it. This measurement shows the circumference of the circle, or the distance around it. Now measure the diameter of the can. Divide the circumference by the diameter to find the value for pi.

The value of pi is a constant. It never changes. It doesn't matter how big a circle is. When you divide the circumference by the diameter, you'll get pi. But what number does pi equal? For any circle, dividing the circumference by the diameter will give 3.14 or $\frac{22}{7}$. This is the value of pi.

For thousands of years, people have worked on finding more and more <u>precise</u> values for pi. You may have used 3.14 as the value in a math class. A more precise value is 3.1415926535897931. In 1844 a German man spent two months finding the first 200 digits of pi. In 1947, D. F. Ferguson raised the number of digits to 808.

Today, using computers, people have found hundreds of millions of digits. Since pi is an irrational number, the digits will never repeat in a pattern. So people who are fascinated can keep working on pi. There will never be a last digit for it.

Main Idea	1		
		Answer	**Score**
	Mark the *main idea*	M	15
	Mark the statement that is *too broad*	B	5
	Mark the statement that is *too narrow*	N	5

a. The value of pi is a constant that we can figure out more and more exactly. ☐ _____

b. The value of pi is 3.1415926535897931. ☐ _____

c. Pi is a constant number. ☐ _____

Score 15 points for each correct answer. Score

Subject Matter 2 This passage is mostly concerned with
☐ a. different parts of circles.
☐ b. figuring out the value of pi.
☐ c. dividing numbers.
☐ d. patterns in numbers. _____

Supporting Details 3 The circumference of a circle is
☐ a. the distance across the center.
☐ b. less than the diameter.
☐ c. always less than 4 units.
☐ d. the distance around the outside. _____

Conclusion 4 From the information in the passage, you can conclude that the value of pi
☐ a. is closer to 3 than to 4.
☐ b. is closer to 4 than to 3.
☐ c. is exactly equal to 3.14.
☐ d. has different values in different situations. _____

Clarifying Devices 5 The writer shows that pi must be less than 4 by
☐ a. describing the history of calculations for pi.
☐ b. explaining what diameter means.
☐ c. using an example.
☐ d. explaining that π is a Greek letter. _____

Vocabulary in Context 6 In this passage, the word precise means
☐ a. difficult.
☐ b. exact.
☐ c. having a pattern.
☐ d. lengthy. _____

Add your scores for questions 1–6. Enter the total here and on the graph on page 158. Total Score _____

8 "Please Excuse My Dear Aunt Sally"

Some students are confused by math problems that contain parentheses. One example is the problem $3(4 + 1)^2 - 8$. What number does this equal? You probably know what the exponent 2 means. When you see that small 2 above the line, it means that a number should be multiplied by itself, or squared. But the problem has other steps in it. The 3 directly in front of the parentheses means you should multiply. The problem also contains addition and subtraction. What should you do first?

To help students grasp this kind of problem, a teacher will explain the order of operations. The steps must be done in a certain order.

To remember the order of the steps, you can use a memory trick. It is the key sentence "Please excuse my dear Aunt Sally." The first letters in the words are PEMDAS. They stand for parentheses, exponents, multiply, divide, add, subtract.

Let's apply the memory trick to the problem above. First do any math inside parentheses. Then use any exponents. Do any multiplying or dividing necessary. Then do any adding or subtracting. Follow the steps to see how this works.

- The math inside the **p**arentheses is to add $4 + 1$. When you do that step, the problem looks like this: $3(5)^2 - 8$
- Next, use the **e**xponent 2. That means multiply 5 by itself. You'll have this result: $3(25) - 8$
- Now **m**ultiply 3 times 25. You will come up with this: $75 - 8$
- **S**ubtract 8 from 75 and you're done: The answer is 67

Of course, this kind of memory <u>device</u> is useless if you can't remember the key sentence. Some students like to create their own sentences, such as "Purple elephants march down a street." What similar memory device can you dream up?

Main Idea	1		
		Answer	**Score**
	Mark the *main idea*	M	15
	Mark the statement that is *too broad*	B	5
	Mark the statement that is *too narrow*	N	5
	a. Math problems can be confusing.	☐	_____
	b. The first step in many problems is to do the math that's in parentheses.	☐	_____
	c. A memory trick can help you remember the order of operations.	☐	_____

Score 15 points for each correct answer.   **Score**

Subject Matter   **2**   This passage is mainly about
☐ a. doing math problems in the right order.
☐ b. making up your own memory tricks.
☐ c. using exponents in math problems.
☐ d. learning how to multiply.   _____

Supporting Details   **3**   The fourth and fifth words in "Please excuse my dear Aunt Sally" remind you to
☐ a. add before you divide.
☐ b. use exponents before you divide.
☐ c. divide before you add.
☐ d. multiply before you divide.   _____

Conclusion   **4**   The last paragraph of the passage is intended to
☐ a. convince you math is easy.
☐ b. make you angry.
☐ c. amuse you.
☐ d. remind you to check your answers to math problems.   _____

Clarifying Devices   **5**   The purpose of the bulleted list in the passage is to
☐ a. introduce the topic.
☐ b. help you understand how to do the problem in the right order.
☐ c. define words like _exponent._
☐ d. teach you how to multiply.   _____

Vocabulary in Context   **6**   In this passage, the word <u>device</u> means
☐ a. to create or make.
☐ b. a loud noise.
☐ c. an adding machine.
☐ d. an aid or tool.   _____

Add your scores for questions 1–6. Enter the total here and on the graph on page 158.   **Total Score**   _____

17

9 The Oldest Math Puzzle

As I was going to St. Ives, I met a man with seven wives.
Every wife had seven sacks, and every sack had seven cats.
Cats, sacks, men, and wives, how many were going to St. Ives?

The *Guinness Book of World Records* tells us that this is the oldest math puzzle. Versions dating from 1650 B.C. have been found. Of course, the very old versions were not in English. Also, the problems may have been about other objects. Every wife could have seven baskets, with seven eggs in each basket. But the key idea of the puzzle remains the same in all the versions.

Most people are tricked by the puzzle for this reason. They start solving it too quickly. They begin multiplying and adding, trying to compute the total number of people and things described. They make a very common math mistake—they do not answer the question. The question asks only how many are going to St. Ives. If you read the puzzle again, you'll see that only one person, the person speaking, is definitely going to St. Ives. The man with the <u>multiplicity</u> of wives, sacks, and cats might be going the opposite direction. He might not be going anywhere at all.

Here is another example. A typical textbook problem might describe a worker packing books in boxes. There are 86 books. He puts 10 books in a box. How many boxes does he need? Dividing 86 by 10 gives the answer 8.6. But that is not the answer to the question. You can't have 8.6 boxes. The answer to the question in the problem is 9 boxes. It is not 8.6 boxes.

The next time you are working a math problem, remember the man going to St. Ives. Be sure you aren't tricked. Read the problem a final time and check that you have answered the correct question.

Main Idea	1		
		Answer	**Score**
	Mark the *main idea*	M	15
	Mark the statement that is *too broad*	B	5
	Mark the statement that is *too narrow*	N	5

a. Be careful to answer the correct question in a math problem. ☐ _____

b. Many math puzzles are thousands of years old. ☐ _____

c. There's no such thing as 8.6 boxes. ☐ _____

Subject Matter   **2**   Which of these is another good title for the passage?
                          ☐ a. Traveling to St. Ives
                          ☐ b. Using Memory Tricks
                          ☐ c. What's the Question?
                          ☐ d. Using Multiplication   _____

Supporting   **3**   The person going to St. Ives
Details   ☐ a. is the speaker in the puzzle.
                          ☐ b. has seven wives.
                          ☐ c. carries a sack.
                          ☐ d. likes to do math problems.   _____

Conclusion   **4**   Which of these statements is a conclusion the
                          author wants you to draw?
                          ☐ a. Sometimes math is a matter of common sense.
                          ☐ b. Old puzzles are usually easy to figure out.
                          ☐ c. Textbooks try to trick students
                          ☐ d. St. Ives no longer exists.   _____

Clarifying   **5**   The first three lines of this passage are in *italic type*
Devices   to
                          ☐ a. help you do the math in them.
                          ☐ b. make them stand out from the regular text.
                          ☐ c. indicate that you should read them twice.
                          ☐ d. indicate that you should memorize them.   _____

Vocabulary   **6**   In this passage, the word <u>multiplicity</u> means
in Context   ☐ a. the answer to a multiplication problem.
                          ☐ b. the opposite of long division.
                          ☐ c. a great many.
                          ☐ d. the wrong number.   _____

Add your scores for questions 1–6. Enter the total here   **Total**
and on the graph on page 158.   **Score**   _____

10 Four out of Five Doctors Recommend . . .

You have probably seen many advertisements for medicines. The ads try to convince you to buy the medicine. They may say, for example, that four out of five doctors recommend a particular headache product. What does this really mean? Exactly how many doctors like the headache medicine? To understand the math behind advertising claims like these, you need to think about how fractions work.

Let's say 500 doctors are in a survey, and 400 of them like the medicine. Then the fraction $\frac{400}{500}$ shows what part of the whole group recommends the product. This fraction is equal to $\frac{4}{5}$. But so are the fractions $\frac{40}{50}$ and $\frac{4000}{5000}$ and even $\frac{40000}{50000}$. So you can't really tell how many doctors were questioned in the survey. All you know is that four out of five said the medicine was good.

So why don't they tell you how many doctors were asked? They could say, "We asked 500 doctors, and 400 of them say the medicine is great." But they don't. Instead they write, "Four out of five doctors recommend our medicine." You aren't told the actual number of doctors in the survey. Maybe they only asked 50. But by telling you four out of five, they may hope you will think that *thousands* of doctors were questioned.

Next time you see an ad that tells you four out of five doctors like a medicine, stop and guess how many doctors that is. You might even write a letter to find out the actual number.

Main Idea   1

	Answer	Score
Mark the *main idea*	**M**	15
Mark the statement that is *too broad*	**B**	5
Mark the statement that is *too narrow*	**N**	5

a. Advertisers use numbers like "four out of five" to mislead people. ☐ _____

a. The fraction $\frac{40}{50}$ is equal to $\frac{4}{5}$. ☐ _____

c. Fractions are sometimes confusing. ☐ _____

Score 15 points for each correct answer.   **Score**

Subject Matter   **2**   Another good title for this passage is
    ☐ a. Reading Labels on Medicine Bottles.
    ☐ b. Why Doctors Recommend Certain Medicines.
    ☐ c. Fractions Always Tell the Truth.
    ☐ d. How Fractions Are Used in Advertising.   _____

Supporting   **3**   A statement like "four out of five"
Details
    ☐ a. always means 40 out of 50 people.
    ☐ b. doesn't tell exactly how many people were
       counted.
    ☐ c. is the fairest way to explain a survey.
    ☐ d. should convince you to buy certain medicines. _____

Conclusion   **4**   The author of this passage thinks you should
    ☐ a. think carefully about ads you hear.
    ☐ b. realize that all ads are full of lies.
    ☐ c. get better at doing math.
    ☐ d. realize that advertisers don't want to mislead
       people.   _____

Clarifying   **5**   The final paragraph of the passage is intended as a
Devices
    ☐ a. criticism of people who don't write letters.
    ☐ b. comparison.
    ☐ c. recommendation.
    ☐ d. joke.   _____

Vocabulary   **6**   In this passage, the word <u>claims</u> means
in Context
    ☐ a. statements that something is true.
    ☐ b. fractions.
    ☐ c. pieces of land belonging to a person.
    ☐ d. lies.   _____

Add your scores for questions 1–6. Enter the total here   **Total**
and on the graph on page 158.   **Score**   _____

11 Not All Pyramids Are Square

The pyramids of Egypt are one of the wonders of the world. Even today no one knows how these impressive monuments were constructed. The Great Pyramid is particularly striking. It is 480 feet high. The base is a square that is 756 feet on each side. It may have taken 4,000 workers 30 years to build this huge structure.

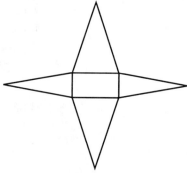

base

Many people think that all pyramids must look like the ones in Egypt. But that is not the case. Pyramids can have many different shapes. The side faces of a pyramid are always triangles. But the base can be some shape other than a square. The base can be a triangle. It can also be a five-sided shape called a pentagon or a six-sided shape called a hexagon. In fact, the base of a pyramid can be any <u>polygon</u>.

Pyramids are named by the shapes of their bases. The Egyptian pyramids are called square pyramids because their bases are squares. But many pyramids aren't square. A triangular pyramid has a triangle for a base. A rectangular pyramid has a rectangle for a base.

Models of pyramids are easy to make. Start by drawing any straight-sided shape. Put triangles on each side. Make each triangle the same height. Cut out the pattern and fold it up. You'll have a model of a pyramid. The drawing at the right shows a rectangle with four triangles around it. When folded, the pattern will make a rectangular pyramid.

Main Idea	1		
		Answer	**Score**
	Mark the *main idea*	M	15
	Mark the statement that is *too broad*	B	5
	Mark the statement that is *too narrow*	N	5
		☐	
	a. The Great Pyramid of Egypt has a square base.	☐	___
	b. Pyramids are named by the shapes of their bases.	☐	___
	c. Pyramids may be huge structures.	☐	___

Subject Matter   **2**   This passage is mostly concerned with
- ☐ a. how long it took to build the Great Pyramid.
- ☐ b. the dimensions of the Great Pyramid.
- ☐ c. how different types of pyramids are named.
- ☐ d. comparing pyramids to squares and cubes.   _____

Supporting Details   **3**   The side faces of a pyramid
- ☐ a. are identical.
- ☐ b. are always triangles.
- ☐ c. are always squares.
- ☐ d. can be different shapes.   _____

Conclusion   **4**   The pyramid in the first diagram is a
- ☐ a. triangular pyramid.
- ☐ b. square pyramid.
- ☐ c. pentagonal pyramid.
- ☐ d. hexagonal pyramid.   _____

Clarifying Devices   **5**   The last paragraph helps you understand pyramids by
- ☐ a. describing the base and side faces.
- ☐ b. comparing them to the pyramids in Egypt.
- ☐ c. explaining how pyramids are named.
- ☐ d. showing you how to build a model.   _____

Vocabulary in Context   **6**   In this passage, the word <u>polygon</u> means
- ☐ a. a flat shape with straight sides.
- ☐ b. a pyramid.
- ☐ c. an Egyptian temple.
- ☐ d. a pattern that can be folded into a pyramid.   _____

Add your scores for questions 1–6. Enter the total here and on the graph on page 158.   **Total Score**   _____

12 Numbers with Personality

Around 550 B.C. a Greek mathematician named Pythagoras founded a center of learning. The teachers and students who joined him were called Pythagoreans. These scholars are given <u>credit</u> for many important discoveries in mathematics. But they also spent time just playing around with number patterns. Some Pythagoreans held the belief that numbers had personality. Even numbers were feminine, while odd numbers were masculine. The number 1 represented reason, and 4 stood for justice. Some numbers were perfect; others were friendly.

These labels for numbers often depended on the number and kinds of divisors. Divisors are numbers that divide into other numbers exactly. For example, 3 is a divisor of 12 because it goes into 12 exactly 4 times. The divisors of 6 are 1, 2, 3, and the number 6 itself. The Pythagoreans called a number perfect if it equaled the sum of all the divisors except for the number itself. Since 6 equals 1 + 2 + 3, 6 is a perfect number.

Are there a lot of perfect numbers? You might think so, but you would be wrong. The next perfect number is 28 (1 + 2 + 4 + 7 + 14). Then come 496, 8128, and 33,550,336. The perfect numbers are rare indeed.

Which numbers were "friendly"? Friendly numbers come in pairs. Each of the two numbers is the sum of the divisors of the other. The divisors of 220 are 1, 2, 4, 5, 10, 11, 20, 22, 44, 55, and 110. Add them together and you get 284. The divisors of 284 are 1, 2, 4, 71, and 142. Their sum is 220. So 220 and 284 are friendly numbers.

Friendly numbers aren't very common either. The tenth such pair, 1184 and 1210, wasn't discovered until 1867. The discovery was made by a 16-year-old boy.

Main Idea	1		
		Answer	**Score**
	Mark the *main idea*	M	15
	Mark the statement that is *too broad*	B	5
	Mark the statement that is *too narrow*	N	5
	a. The Pythagoreans classified numbers in several different ways.	☐	___
	b. Many numbers have interesting qualities.	☐	___
	c. There are only a few pairs of friendly numbers.	☐	___

Score 15 points for each correct answer.   **Score**

Subject Matter 2 This passage is mainly about
- ☐ a. Pythagoras.
- ☐ b. how the Pythagoreans classified numbers.
- ☐ c. what a divisor is.
- ☐ d. practical uses for perfect and friendly numbers. _____

Supporting Details 3 The Pythagoreans thought that odd numbers such as 3 and 11 were
- ☐ a. perfect.
- ☐ b. friendly.
- ☐ c. feminine.
- ☐ d. masculine. _____

Conclusion 4 Perfect numbers are
- ☐ a. always greater than 100.
- ☐ b. always less than one million.
- ☐ c. rare and difficult to find.
- ☐ d. common and easy to find. _____

Clarifying Devices 5 The information in the last sentence is intended to
- ☐ a. surprise you.
- ☐ b. prove that math is easy.
- ☐ c. confuse you.
- ☐ d. convince you to like number patterns. _____

Vocabulary in Context 6 In this passage, the word <u>credit</u> means
- ☐ a. money.
- ☐ b. honor.
- ☐ c. trust.
- ☐ d. blame. _____

Add your scores for questions 1–6. Enter the total here and on the graph on page 158.   **Total Score** _____

13 The "Right" Angle

What is the "right" angle? It depends, of course, on what you need the angle for. However, in mathematics, a right angle is one with a very specific size.

An angle is formed whenever two straight lines come together at a point. The size of an angle is the distance between the lines, *not* the lengths of the lines. Angles are measured in degrees using a tool called a protractor. This tool is a <u>semicircular</u> piece of plastic or metal marked in degrees. A protractor can be used to measure or to draw an angle of any desired size.

So what is a right angle? It is an angle that measures 90 degrees. One way to visualize a right angle is to think about a square or a rectangle, familiar four-sided geometric shapes. The angle in each corner of a square or rectangle is a right angle. If you cut a square in half from one corner to the opposite corner, you'll get two triangles. Each of them is a right triangle because each has one right angle. Many geometric figures have one or more right angles.

Angles that are not right angles have special names. Angles less than 90 degrees are acute angles. Angles greater than 90 degrees are obtuse angles. A triangular "Yield" sign has three acute angles. The eight-sided "Stop" sign has eight obtuse angles.

Once you start looking for right angles, you'll find them everywhere. Windows, doors, walls, and tables all make use of right angles. If the angles aren't right, the objects look crooked. If the legs of a table don't make right angles with the top, the table will wobble. In many types of construction projects, the only "right" angle is a right angle!

Main Idea	1		
		Answer	Score
Mark the *main idea*		M	15
Mark the statement that is *too broad*		B	5
Mark the statement that is *too narrow*		N	5

a. A protractor is used to measure angles.	☐	___
b. Many objects contain angles.	☐	___
c. Right angles—angles measuring 90 degrees—are found frequently in the everyday world.	☐	___

Score 15 points for each correct answer.   **Score**

Subject Matter   2   This passage is mainly about
      ☐ a. how to measure angles.
      ☐ b. the definition of and uses for a right angle.
      ☐ c. angles measuring more than 90 degrees.
      ☐ d. squares, rectangles, and triangles.   _____

Supporting   3   An acute angle
Details
      ☐ a. measures 90 degrees.
      ☐ b. measures more than 90 degrees.
      ☐ c. measures less than 90 degrees.
      ☐ d. is formed whenever two lines meet at a point.   _____

Conclusion   4   It is logical to conclude that
      ☐ a. nearly all angles are right angles.
      ☐ b. no one uses a protractor anymore.
      ☐ c. right angles are found in trees and other
          growing things.
      ☐ d. engineers, architects, and construction
          workers use right angles.   _____

Clarifying   5   The writer helps you visualize different kinds of
Devices   angles by
      ☐ a. giving examples of places they are used.
      ☐ b. describing what a table looks like.
      ☐ c. asking several questions.
      ☐ d. telling what a protractor is.   _____

Vocabulary   6   Semicircular means shaped like
in Context
      ☐ a. an oval.
      ☐ b. a full moon.
      ☐ c. half a circle.
      ☐ d. two circles.   _____

Add your scores for questions 1–6. Enter the total here   **Total**
and on the graph on page 158.   **Score**   _____

14 A Theorem Most Proved

A theorem is a math statement that has been proved true. If you have taken high school mathematics classes, you have <u>undoubtedly</u> studied or even proved theorems. The most frequently proved theorem of all time is probably one called the Pythagorean Theorem. All mathematicians know that the theorem is true. But many people, including United States President James Garfield, have entertained themselves by creating new proofs for this theorem. One book published in 1940 had more than 370 different proofs.

To understand the Pythagorean Theorem, you need to know only two things: how to square a number and the definition of a right triangle. To square a number means to multiply it by itself. The square of 3 is 3 times 3, or 9. Four squared is 16; 5 squared equals 25. A right triangle must have one right angle, an angle measuring 90 degrees. (You might remember that a right angle looks like the corner of a square.)

So, what does the Pythagorean Theorem say? It states that if you add the squares of the two short sides of a right triangle, the sum is equal to the square of the longest side. The triangle in the drawing has short sides of 3 and 4 units. Three squared is 9; four squared is 16; the sum of 9 and 16 is 25. And 25 equals the square of the long side, 5 times 5. This theorem holds true for all right triangles.

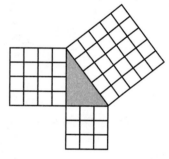

One use of this idea is in making a right angle. If you cut three pieces of wood and make them 3 feet, 4 feet, and 5 feet long, you can construct a triangle. According to the Pythagorean Theorem, this must be a right triangle. Cutting wood to these lengths is one way people create a right angle for construction or engineering projects.

Main Idea   1 ───

	Answer	Score
Mark the *main idea*	M	15
Mark the statement that is *too broad*	B	5
Mark the statement that is *too narrow*	N	5

a. The Pythagorean Theorem tells how the sides of a right triangle are related.	☐	____
b. President Garfield wrote a proof of the Pythagorean Theorem.	☐	____
c. Many theorems in math have more than one proof.	☐	____

Score 15 points for each correct answer.   **Score**

Subject Matter 2   This passage is mainly about
- [ ] a. squaring numbers.
- [ ] b. the Pythagorean Theorem.
- [ ] c. triangles and their uses.
- [ ] d. constructing right angles from wood.   _____

Supporting Details 3   A right triangle has an angle of
- [ ] a. 30 degrees.
- [ ] b. 50 degrees.
- [ ] c. 90 degrees.
- [ ] d. 120 degrees.   _____

Conclusion 4   The diagram in the passage is intended to
- [ ] a. show what a square looks like.
- [ ] b. show that 3 plus 4 can equal 5.
- [ ] c. prove that not all triangles are right triangles.
- [ ] d. illustrate the Pythagorean Theorem.   _____

Clarifying Devices 5   In the last paragraph, the writer describes a
- [ ] a. right triangle.
- [ ] b. proof of the Pythagorean Theorem.
- [ ] c. practical use of the Pythagorean Theorem.
- [ ] d. construction project.   _____

Vocabulary in Context 6   Undoubtedly means
- [ ] a. without a doubt.
- [ ] b. causing doubt.
- [ ] c. full of doubt.
- [ ] d. afraid of doubt.   _____

Add your scores for questions 1–6. Enter the total here and on the graph on page 158.   **Total Score**   _____

15 Distances and Light Years

You've probably measured length with a ruler. You may have used inches as the unit of measurement, or you may have used centimeters. There are many different units used to measure length. In addition to inches and centimeters, there are feet, yards, miles, and kilometers.

But how are *really* long distances measured? For example, the average distance from Earth to the sun is about 93 million miles. Distances like this one are not measured, of course. No one takes a long tape measure and stretches it from Earth to the sun! These types of distances are computed using other mathematical quantities.

Distances outside our solar system can be really huge. The nearest star, Proxima Centauri, is 25 trillion miles away. Written out, this distance is 25,000,000,000,000 miles. These very large numbers become difficult to write and use. So, in the late 1880s, scientists invented a very large unit of measure. They called it the light year. This is the distance that light travels in one solar year, 365 days.

Light travels very quickly indeed. The speed of light is about 186,000 miles per second. Light from the moon gets to us in 1.25 seconds, whereas light from the sun takes about 8.25 minutes. Even from Pluto, the most distant planet in our solar system, it takes about 6 hours for light to travel the distance to Earth. In 365 days, light travels about 5.9 trillion miles. So a light year was defined to be that distance. The term *light year* is a little misleading because a light year is a measure of distance, not time.

In light years, the distance from us to Proxima Centauri is 4.2. The brightest star, Sirius, is 8.7 light years distant. Light years turn <u>astronomical</u> distances into smaller numbers. These numbers are easier to use and remember.

Main Idea 1

	Answer	Score
Mark the *main idea*	M	15
Mark the statement that is *too broad*	B	5
Mark the statement that is *too narrow*	N	5

a. It is 25 trillion miles to the nearest star. ☐ ___

b. It can be interesting to study facts about stars and planets. ☐ ___

c. Light years are used to measure very long distances. ☐ ___

Subject Matter　2　This passage is mainly about
- [ ] a. measuring distances to stars.
- [ ] b. the solar system.
- [ ] c. different types of stars.
- [ ] d. the distance from Earth to the sun.　　____

Supporting Details　3　A light year is a distance equal to about
- [ ] a. 93 million miles.
- [ ] b. 25 trillion miles.
- [ ] c. 365 days.
- [ ] d. 5.9 trillion miles.　　____

Conclusion　4　The distance from Earth to the moon is usually not described in light years because this distance
- [ ] a. is too long.
- [ ] b. is too short.
- [ ] c. changes at different times of the year.
- [ ] d. has not yet been measured accurately.　　____

Clarifying Devices　5　In the first paragraph, the writer
- [ ] a. explains how to use a ruler.
- [ ] b. mentions familiar units of measurement.
- [ ] c. describes different stars in the night sky.
- [ ] d. defines the speed of light.　　____

Vocabulary in Context　6　In this passage, the word <u>astronomical</u> means
- [ ] a. scientific.
- [ ] b. amazing.
- [ ] c. having to do with stars and planets.
- [ ] d. having to do with measuring.　　____

Add your scores for questions 1–6. Enter the total here and on the graph on page 158.　　Total Score　____

16 Sherlock Holmes Solves a Math Problem

Doing mathematics is much like solving a mystery. If a math problem is challenging, you may look for clues, try different approaches, or start by gathering data. Above all, you need logical reasoning.

One of the most famous logical reasoners of all is the fictional character Sherlock Holmes. In the stories and novels of Arthur Conan Doyle, Holmes and his loyal friend Watson solve a wide variety of mysteries. Holmes considers detection a science. When Watson reports their adventures, Holmes can be impatient if Watson emphasizes the exciting drama more than the pure logic.

"The Adventure of the Musgrave Ritual" is a typical Sherlock Holmes story. In the story, facts seem to lead to a hidden treasure. Holmes realizes that he needs to find the end of the shadow of an elm tree at a certain time. However, the elm has been cut down. Another character remembers that the elm was 64 feet tall. So Holmes uses a six-foot fishing pole and a little math. The six-foot pole casts a shadow nine feet long. Holmes draws a diagram like the one at the right, showing the pole and its shadow. Holmes knows that the shadow of the

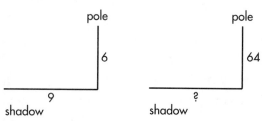

tree will be <u>proportionally</u> as long as the shadow of the pole. Doing a little math, he figures that the shadow of the 64-foot tree was 96 feet long.

The next time you have a difficult math problem to do, remember Sherlock Holmes. He found his math skills useful in his work. Someday you may too.

Main Idea   1

	Answer	Score
Mark the *main idea*	M	15
Mark the statement that is *too broad*	B	5
Mark the statement that is *too narrow*	N	5

a. Sherlock Holmes once used mathematics to solve a mystery. ☐ _____

b. Math has many uses in real life. ☐ _____

c. Holmes needed to find the length of the elm tree's shadow. ☐ _____

Score 15 points for each correct answer.   Score

Subject Matter 2 Another good title for this passage would be
- [ ] a. Drawing a Picture.
- [ ] b. How Long Was the Shadow?
- [ ] c. Solving Mysteries.
- [ ] d. Measuring a Fishing Pole.   _____

Supporting Details 3 In the math problem described in the passage, Sherlock Holmes wants to find the
- [ ] a. time at which an elm tree was cut down.
- [ ] b. length of the shadow of a 6-foot pole.
- [ ] c. height of an elm that is no longer there.
- [ ] d. length of the shadow of an elm that is no longer there.   _____

Conclusion 4 The missing number in the diagram should be
- [ ] a. 6
- [ ] b. 9.
- [ ] c. 64.
- [ ] d. 96.   _____

Clarifying Devices 5 The writer points out an everyday use of math by
- [ ] a. giving facts about shadows.
- [ ] b. telling about Arthur Conan Doyle's life.
- [ ] c. explaining how to solve a murder mystery.
- [ ] d. telling a story.   _____

Vocabulary in Context 6 In this passage, the word proportionally has to do with
- [ ] a. one object in relation to another.
- [ ] b. opposites.
- [ ] c. lengths.
- [ ] d. surprises.   _____

Add your scores for questions 1–6. Enter the total here and on the graph on page 158.

Total Score   _____

33

17 The Fastest Answer

Carl Friedrich Gauss, one of the most famous of all mathematicians, was born in Germany in 1777. Gauss made contributions to physics and astronomy as well as to mathematics. He was a child <u>prodigy</u>, making many important discoveries before the age of 20. As early as three years old, Gauss corrected his father's math when he was adding a series of long computations.

In his later years, Gauss liked to tell a story from his school days. When he was 10, he entered his first arithmetic class. The teacher was particularly strict, perhaps even cruel. In one beginning class, he gave the boys a very difficult addition problem, a list of 100 numbers to be added. The problem may have looked like this:

$$4897 + 4970 + 5043 + \ldots + 12{,}124$$

At that time, school boys did their math on small slates using chalk. The first boy to solve a problem was to lay his slate on the teacher's desk. As each boy finished, he added to the stack of slates. The teacher had barely finished writing the problem when Gauss wrote down the answer and laid his slate on the desk. As the other boys worked on the problem for the next hour, Gauss sat quietly and ignored the sarcastic glances from his teacher. Of course, Gauss had the right answer; in fact, he was the only student who got the long and difficult problem correct.

How did he do it? He had looked at the numbers and seen a pattern in them. In this case, each number to be added was 73 more than the preceding number. In any series of this type, a formula can be applied to the numbers to quickly arrive at a solution. Although the formula is a rather simple part of mathematics, the child Gauss made the initial discovery of it at the age of 10!

Main Idea	1		
		Answer	**Score**
	Mark the *main idea*	M	15
	Mark the statement that is *too broad*	B	5
	Mark the statement that is *too narrow*	N	5

a. The mathematician Gauss showed his talents at a very early age. ☐ _____

b. Gauss added the series of large numbers quickly. ☐ _____

c. Some mathematicians are remarkably intelligent. ☐ _____

Score 15 points for each correct answer. Score

Subject Matter 2 This passage is mostly concerned with
☐ a. the contributions Gauss made to mathematics.
☐ b. an early incident in the life of Gauss.
☐ c. how to add a long series of numbers.
☐ d. methods of education in the 1700s. _____

Supporting 3 Gauss solved the difficult math problem by
Details ☐ a. using a computer.
☐ b. making a diagram.
☐ c. carefully adding all the numbers.
☐ d. figuring out a formula. _____

Conclusion 4 Gauss's teacher probably assumed that
☐ a. students would solve the problem by cheating.
☐ b. everyone in the class enjoyed math.
☐ c. it would take all the students a long time to solve the problem.
☐ d. few of the students knew how to add. _____

Clarifying 5 The writer describes Gauss's amazing talents by
Devices ☐ a. relating a story.
☐ b. explaining a math problem.
☐ c. comparing him to other mathematicians.
☐ d. describing his key discoveries. _____

Vocabulary 6 The word <u>prodigy</u> means a
in Context ☐ a. student.
☐ b. very brilliant young person.
☐ c. teacher.
☐ d. parent. _____

Add your scores for questions 1–6. Enter the total here Total
and on the graph on page 158. Score _____

18 Proving Fermat's Last Theorem

The statement, found scribbled in the margin of a book, has been the most tantalizing statement in higher mathematics. Elementary school students learn the Pythagorean theorem: $a^2 + b^2 = c^2$. Fermat's statement is related to the Pythagorean theorem, but it is a negative statement. It says that $a^3 + b^3$ does *not* equal c^3, and that, furthermore, the equation is just as invalid whenever the exponent is above 2. So $a^4 + b^4$ never equals c^4, $a^5 + b^5$ never equals c^5, and so on.

The margin note had been left by eminent 17th-century mathematician Pierre de Fermat, and it contended that he had discovered a proof for his conjecture—but that there was not enough room to write it in the margin. Fermat's statement intrigued and challenged mathematicians for the next 300 years, for no one could prove it. In higher mathematics, it is not sufficient merely to state that a theorem is true because it holds true for every number that you try it with; you must devise a proof that can be demonstrated to work with *any* possible number inserted into the equation. A statement has little or no value until such a proof is substantiated.

Fermat's Last Theorem, as it was called, was the most significant unproved theorem in higher mathematics, and it was not conclusively demonstrated to be true until 1994. At that time, mathematician Andrew Wiles, who had spent years struggling with the problem, corrected his 1993 proof, and his astonished colleagues certified his work as legitimate.

At 150 pages, however, Wiles's proof is certainly not the same proof that Fermat envisioned centuries ago. In that respect, Fermat's marginal note will remain an <u>enigma</u> forever.

Main Idea	1		
		Answer	**Score**
Mark the *main idea*		M	15
Mark the statement that is *too broad*		B	5
Mark the statement that is *too narrow*		N	5
a. Many mathematical theorems are difficult to prove.		☐	_____
b. Fermat's famous theorem was not absolutely proved for hundreds of years.		☐	_____
c. Fermat's theorem says that $a^3 + b^3$ does not equal c^3.		☐	_____

Score 15 points for each correct answer.   Score

Subject Matter 2 This passage is mostly concerned with
- ☐ a. why mathematical proofs fascinate some people.
- ☐ b. the life of Pierre de Fermat.
- ☐ c. Fermat's theorem and the difficulties of proving it.
- ☐ d. how Andrew Wiles proved Fermat's theorem. _____

Supporting Details 3 Fermat's theorem was not proved for
- ☐ a. 200 years.
- ☐ b. 300 years.
- ☐ c. 400 years.
- ☐ d. 500 years. _____

Conclusion 4 It seems logical to assume that Andrew Wiles
- ☐ a. loved a challenge.
- ☐ b. was very arrogant.
- ☐ c. was disliked by his colleagues.
- ☐ d. came up with the same proof that Fermat had in mind. _____

Clarifying Devices 5 The writer helps the reader to understand Fermat's theorem by
- ☐ a. comparing it to the Pythagorean theorem.
- ☐ b. showing how Andrew Wiles proved it.
- ☐ c. telling about the famous marginal note.
- ☐ d. explaining why theorems must be proved. _____

Vocabulary in Context 6 The word <u>enigma</u> means
- ☐ a. proof.
- ☐ b. theorem.
- ☐ c. untruth.
- ☐ d. mystery. _____

Add your scores for questions 1–6. Enter the total here and on the graph on page 158.   Total Score _____

19 Working with Interest Rates

When you put money in a bank account, your money earns interest. This interest is a payment from the bank for the use of your money. The bank may pay you any interest rate it desires; these days the usual rate is around 5 percent. The basic formula for figuring out how much interest you will earn on an investment is fairly simple. To figure the interest, multiply three things: the **p**rincipal (or amount you invest), the interest **r**ate put into decimal form (5 percent would be written .05), and the **t**ime in years. The formula can be written as $i = prt$.

The formula $i = prt$ is for simple interest. It does not help you find interest that is compounded. Compounding occurs when you leave your money alone. Then every so often the interest is computed again using a new principal. The formula for compound interest lets you find the value of an investment after some number of years. However, it is a fairly complex formula. If you want to work with it, you'll need a scientific calculator with an exponent key.

Most people find the compound interest formula <u>perplexing</u>. They ask a bank or other investment service to do the math for them. But there is a simple way to figure out when your money will double in value. This is called the "Rule of 72." If you divide the annual interest rate into 72, the answer is the number of years it will take to double your savings. So money invested at 5 percent will take more than 14 years to double (72 divided by 5).

Now here is a question to ponder. What happens if p equals zero? If you put that value for p into the formula, the answer will be zero. In other words, if you invest no principal, you'll get no interest. And although this is the simplest math of all, it is not a good long-term investment strategy!

Main Idea	1		
		Answer	**Score**
Mark the _main idea_		M	15
Mark the statement that is _too broad_		B	5
Mark the statement that is _too narrow_		N	5

a. Calculating interest from investments is based on formulas and rules. ☐ _____

b. Compound interest formulas are very complicated. ☐ _____

c. Investment strategies require math. ☐ _____

Subject Matter   **2**   This passage is mostly about
- ☐ a. understanding mathematical formulas.
- ☐ b. why saving money is important.
- ☐ c. ways to figure out how much money you are earning in a bank account.
- ☐ d. using a scientific calculator.   _____

Supporting Details   **3**   The "Rule of 72" helps you find the
- ☐ a. current interest rate.
- ☐ b. interest you get after 72 years.
- ☐ c. amount of money you should invest.
- ☐ d. number of years it takes an investment to double in value.   _____

Conclusion   **4**   At 7 percent annual interest, an investment will double in about
- ☐ a. 10 months.
- ☐ b. 10 years.
- ☐ c. 72 months.
- ☐ d. 72 years.   _____

Clarifying Devices   **5**   Letters are underlined in three words in the first paragraph in order to show that
- ☐ a. the letters are part of the interest formula.
- ☐ b. the letters should be capitalized.
- ☐ c. the words they are in are spelled incorrectly.
- ☐ d. each letter stands for a number.   _____

Vocabulary in Context   **6**   Perplexing means
- ☐ a. unnecessary.
- ☐ b. long.
- ☐ c. confusing.
- ☐ d. involving percents.   _____

Add your scores for questions 1–6. Enter the total here and on the graph on page 158.   **Total Score**   _____

20 The Bridges of Königsberg

The city of Königsberg, Germany, has seven bridges and a river. The bridges connect an island with other parts of the town. For many years, people argued about the bridges. Was it possible to walk through the city and cross each bridge only once? Many people tried it. But they either skipped a bridge or crossed a bridge more than once.

The Swiss mathematician Leonhard Euler heard about the puzzle of the bridges. He thought it was an interesting problem. Euler <u>reduced</u> the problem to its most basic elements. He drew a diagram that showed only the seven bridges. Such a diagram is called a *network*. Then he tried to trace the diagram with a pencil without retracing any part of the diagram.

Here is a network showing the bridges of Königsberg. There are seven heavy dark bands, one for each bridge. It is much easier to try to trace the network with a pencil than to walk around the city trying to find a route over the bridges.

Euler was able to prove that there is no solution to the problem. A route that included each bridge once and only once was impossible. As Euler worked on the problem, he discovered other more general things about networks. He wrote several important theorems that mathematicians use to analyze all types of networks.

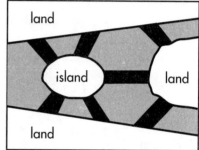

Today networks are used to represent many kinds of situations. The part of mathematics that began with the puzzle of the Königsberg bridges may now be helping you to make a long-distance telephone call or to sign on to the Internet.

Main Idea 1

	Answer	Score
Mark the *main idea*	M	15
Mark the statement that is *too broad*	B	5
Mark the statement that is *too narrow*	N	5

a. Königsberg has seven bridges. ☐ _____

b. The mathematics of networks began with a puzzle about bridges. ☐ _____

c. Networks may help you make a long distance call. ☐ _____

Subject Matter   **2**   This passage is mostly concerned with
- [ ] a. the life of the mathematician Leonhard Euler.
- [ ] b. the city of Königsberg, Germany.
- [ ] c. networks and how they are used.
- [ ] d. why some math problems have no solution.   _____

Supporting Details   **3**   Leonhard Euler used a network to prove that
- [ ] a. all networks have seven lines.
- [ ] b. the bridges could not be crossed only once in one trip across the city.
- [ ] c. the problem of the bridges was incorrectly stated.
- [ ] d. networks are needed for telephone cables.   _____

Conclusion   **4**   In the network diagram, the gray areas stand for
- [ ] a. bridges.
- [ ] b. the river.
- [ ] c. a road.
- [ ] d. land.   _____

Clarifying Devices   **5**   In the first paragraph, the writer introduces the concept of networks by
- [ ] a. explaining a mathematical diagram.
- [ ] b. giving a short biography of Leonhard Euler.
- [ ] c. describing an old puzzle about bridges.
- [ ] d. relating networks to telephone cable systems.   _____

Vocabulary in Context   **6**   In this passage, <u>reduced</u> means
- [ ] a. simplified.
- [ ] b. lost weight.
- [ ] c. lessened the amount of.
- [ ] d. figured out again.   _____

Add your scores for questions 1–6. Enter the total here and on the graph on page 158.   **Total Score**   _____

21 The Better Buy

Many consumer products come in more than one size. We all assume that you save money if you buy the largest size you can use, and most of the time this assumption turns out to be true. Sometimes, however, the savings may not be <u>significant</u>. So before you automatically reach for the largest size of some product, you might want to do a little math.

Assume a product comes in two sizes: the smaller size has 24 ounces and costs $1.19; the larger size has 36 ounces and costs $1.69. To find the savings, if any, on the larger size, you can compute the unit price. (Units are ounces, pounds, or whatever measure the product is sold in.) In this case, the unit price is the cost per ounce for each size, so use a calculator to divide the price by the number of ounces.

24 ounces for $1.19 $1.19 ÷ 24 ounces = 0.0495 = 4.95¢ per ounce
36 ounces for $1.69 $1.69 ÷ 36 ounces = 0.0469 = 4.69¢ per ounce

You can see that the 36 ounce-size has a lower unit price, so it is the better buy.

But how much do you actually save by buying the larger size? To find out, subtract the two unit prices to compare them: $0.0495 − $0.0469 = $0.0026. In this example, the difference in the unit prices is about $0.003—only three-tenths of a penny! So if you don't really need the larger size of this particular product, you probably shouldn't purchase it. In addition to price, another factor to consider when choosing the size to buy is the expiration date on the product. If you're not likely to use up the larger size before the expiration date, then you should buy a smaller size.

The next time you go to the supermarket, take a pocket calculator with you and try finding the unit prices on different sizes of some products. You may very well discover that a *smaller* size offers you the best value!

Main Idea	1		
		Answer	Score
Mark the *main idea*		M	15
Mark the statement that is *too broad*		B	5
Mark the statement that is *too narrow*		N	5

a. A pocket calculator can help in computing the unit price. ☐ ____

b. Mathematics can help consumers. ☐ ____

c. Computing unit prices helps you compare costs. ☐ ____

Subject Matter   **2**   This passage is mainly about
- ☐ a. using a calculator.
- ☐ b. comparison shopping.
- ☐ c. balancing a household budget.
- ☐ d. dividing decimals.   _____

Supporting Details   **3**   To compute a unit price, you should
- ☐ a. first change ounces to pounds.
- ☐ b. subtract two numbers.
- ☐ c. divide the price by the expiration date.
- ☐ d. divide the price by the number of units.   _____

Conclusion   **4**   It is reasonable to conclude that you
- ☐ a. never save money buying a larger size.
- ☐ b. always save money buying a larger size.
- ☐ c. may not save much money buying a larger size.
- ☐ d. usually don't use a product before it expires.   _____

Clarifying Devices   **5**   The writer shows how to compare prices for
- ☐ a. two different sizes of the same product.
- ☐ b. two different brands of the same product.
- ☐ c. products without price labels.
- ☐ d. products that are sold at farmers' markets.   _____

Vocabulary in Context   **6**   In this passage, the word <u>significant</u> means
- ☐ a. able to be printed on a sign.
- ☐ b. practical.
- ☐ c. large enough to make a difference.
- ☐ d. important.   _____

Add your scores for questions 1–6. Enter the total here and on the graph on page 158.   **Total Score**   _____

22 Bits and Bytes

Even though the workings of computers appear complicated, in essence a computer understands only two things—on and off. So all information is presented to the computer in terms of just two digits, 0 and 1. In computer language, these are *bits*. The word *bit* is short for **bi**nary dig**it**. A sequence of eight bits—for example, 01001010—is a *byte*.

Because the computer only needs two numbers to operate, it uses a number system called base 2, or binary. Just as the number system we normally use, base 10, has ten digits (0, 1, 2, 3, 4, 5, 6, 7, 8, and 9), base 2 has two digits (0 and 1). This makes for some very long numbers; for example, in base 2 the number 45 is written 101101!

Words used by computer scientists may have meanings that are different from the meanings you <u>anticipate</u>. This is because binary numbers are so vital to computer science. You might suppose that a kilobyte equals 1,000 bytes—after all, the prefix *kilo-* means "one thousand" in words such as *kilometer* and *kilogram*. But a kilobyte does not equal one thousand bytes; it equals 1,024 bytes. The reason for this goes back to the way the binary number system functions. Similarly, a megabyte does not equal one million bytes, even though *mega-* means "million." A megabyte is actually 1,048,576 bytes.

The next time you operate a computer, you might try looking at its basic information panel and checking the memory. It might tell you that you have 624 megabytes of available memory. So what does that really mean? How many bits can the computer store with that much memory? Now that you know about bits and bytes, you can multiply to find out. Put the number of megabytes into this equation: $N \times 1,048,576 \times 8$. If N stands for 624 megabytes, the answer is 5,234,491,392 bits. That's enough 1s and 0s to reach across the entire United States!

Main Idea	1		
		Answer	**Score**
	Mark the *main idea*	M	15
	Mark the statement that is *too broad*	B	5
	Mark the statement that is *too narrow*	N	5
	a. A byte is eight bits.	☐	____
	b. Computers run on a base two, or binary, number system.	☐	____
	c. Number systems are interesting.	☐	____

Subject Matter 2 This passage is mostly concerned with explaining
- ☐ a. the way the binary number system works.
- ☐ b. what base ten means.
- ☐ c. how bits and bytes work in computers.
- ☐ d. the meaning of the prefixes *kilo-* and *mega-*. _____

Supporting Details 3 Most of the time, the prefix *kilo-* means
- ☐ a. a unit for measuring distance.
- ☐ b. one thousand.
- ☐ c. 1024.
- ☐ d. one million. _____

Conclusion 4 You can conclude from the final paragraph that
- ☐ a. computers can store a great deal of information.
- ☐ b. most computers do not have enough memory.
- ☐ c. you need to be able to multiply large numbers to use a computer.
- ☐ d. a kilobyte is larger than a megabyte. _____

Clarifying Devices 5 The passage discusses binary numbers in order to
- ☐ a. show that 45 can be written in two different ways.
- ☐ b. explain how computers operate.
- ☐ c. explain kilobytes.
- ☐ d. explain megabytes. _____

Vocabulary in Context 6 In this passage, the word <u>anticipate</u> means
- ☐ a. expect.
- ☐ b. look forward to.
- ☐ c. forget.
- ☐ d. remember. _____

Add your scores for questions 1–6. Enter the total here and on the graph on page 158. **Total Score** _____

23 Shapes That Cover

Probably somewhere in your home you have a floor or wall covered with square tiles. The majority of homes have a tile pattern somewhere, usually in kitchens and bathrooms. Have you ever thought about the geometry of tiled surfaces? Why are squares used so often? Can other geometric shapes such as triangles and circles be used equally well?

It turns out that not all shapes can be used to completely cover a flat surface. A covering over a flat surface is called a *tessellation* in mathematics. It is a complete covering with no holes and no overlaps. Squares will tessellate a surface, but circles won't. Another shape that works is a regular hexagon. This six-sided shape is seen in floor tiles as well as in such materials as chicken wire.

Another familiar tessellation is one made from rectangular bricks that are about 4 inches long and 8 inches wide. Why does this shape work well to cover a surface? This rectangle is actually two squares put together. Any rectangle twice as long as it is wide will work for this tessellation. The diagram shows one possible arrangement. If you take a pencil and divide each rectangle into two squares, you'll see the square grid that <u>underlies</u> the tiling.

Once you starting looking for tessellation patterns, you will observe them in many places. You might keep a sketchbook of the possibilities you notice in walls, brick paths, and floors. Then, the next time you are planning to tile a floor or wall, you'll have choices other than plain old boring squares!

Main Idea 1 ——————————————————————

	Answer	Score
Mark the *main idea*	M	15
Mark the statement that is *too broad*	B	5
Mark the statement that is *too narrow*	N	5
a. Geometry helps to cover floors.	☐	____
b. Various geometric shapes can be used to cover a floor or wall.	☐	____
c. Squares and hexagons will tesselate a surface.	☐	____

Subject Matter 2 This passage is mainly about
- ☐ a. rectangles twice as long as they are wide.
- ☐ b. different kinds of tile patterns that will completely cover a surface.
- ☐ c. how to choose a type of floor for a kitchen or bathroom.
- ☐ d. floor coverings using six-sided pieces.

_____

Supporting Details 3 One geometric shape that _cannot_ be used in a tessellation is a
- ☐ a. square.
- ☐ b. rectangle.
- ☐ c. circle.
- ☐ d. hexagon.

_____

Conclusion 4 It is reasonable to conclude that
- ☐ a. squares and rectangles are often used in tessellations.
- ☐ b. rectangular tiles cost more than square tiles.
- ☐ c. a hexagon is a five-sided figure.
- ☐ d. it is hard to lay out a floor with a tesselation.

_____

Clarifying Devices 5 The writer explains tessellations through
- ☐ a. descriptions and a diagram.
- ☐ b. comparisons and instructions.
- ☐ c. formulas and procedures.
- ☐ d. explaining how to draw them.

_____

Vocabulary in Context 6 In this passage, the word <u>underlies</u> means
- ☐ a. keeps the pieces separated.
- ☐ b. rests comfortably.
- ☐ c. forms the foundation of.
- ☐ d. is used as a glue.

_____

Add your scores for questions 1–6. Enter the total here and on the graph on page 158.

Total Score

_____

24 Using Exchange Rates

Are you—or is someone you know—planning a trip outside the United States? If so, it may be necessary to use math skills when making purchases. Each country has a different form of money, and a traveler will want to know how much a product or meal costs in U.S. dollars.

To convert foreign money, a traveler needs to know the current exchange rate. This is a number that helps a person figure out how the foreign <u>currency</u> translates into dollars. Exchange rates for foreign currencies change all the time. They depend on how much a nation's money is in demand by other nations. Currency values were once based on the value of gold, but now they are set by international agreements.

Exchange rates are found in the business sections of most newspapers. For example, currency in Denmark is called *kroner.* You might find that one dollar currently equals 6.61 Danish kroner. To change dollars to kroner, multiply by 6.61. To change kroner to dollars, divide by 6.61. Since doing this type of arithmetic in a crowded souvenir shop, even with a calculator, might be difficult, many people use a conversion table. Before you leave on your trip, make a table like the one shown below. You can use your table to estimate the dollar amount of an item you'd like to buy. For example, an item marked as 130 kroner will cost between $15 and $20. Doing a little practice ahead of time can help you stick to your travel budget. Being prepared may also prevent unpleasant surprises when your charge card bill arrives!

Dollars	Kroner	Dollars	Kroner	Dollars	Kroner	Dollars	Kroner
$1	6.61	$15	99.15	$40	264.40	$70	462.70
$2	13.22	$20	132.20	$45	297.45	$80	528.80
$5	33.05	$25	165.25	$50	330.50	$90	594.90
$10	66.10	$30	198.30	$60	396.60	$100	661.00

Main Idea   1

	Answer	Score
Mark the *main idea*	**M**	15
Mark the statement that is *too broad*	**B**	5
Mark the statement that is *too narrow*	**N**	5

a. Exchange rates can be used to convert one country's money into another's. ☐ _____

b. Exchange rates are set by international agreements. ☐ _____

c. Some travel requires different forms of money. ☐ _____

Score 15 points for each correct answer.   **Score**

Subject Matter   **2**   This passage is mainly concerned with
☐ a. comparing U.S. and Danish money.
☐ b. spending money when traveling outside the United States.
☐ c. how money values are decided on.
☐ d. estimating prices when traveling outside the United States.   _____

Supporting Details   **3**   Exchange rates for foreign monies
☐ a. never change.
☐ b. change frequently.
☐ c. can only be found in travel guidebooks.
☐ d. are always given in kroner.   _____

Conclusion   **4**   From the information in this passage, it is reasonable to conclude that German money
☐ a. has a value that changes often.
☐ b. has the same exchange rate as Danish money.
☐ c. cannot be converted into American money.
☐ d. has a value that keeps going up.   _____

Clarifying Devices   **5**   The table in the passage is intended as a help for
☐ a. buying inexpensive souvenirs.
☐ b. figuring out the price of an item when it is given in Danish kroner.
☐ c. figuring out distances in Denmark.
☐ d. bargaining down a price in Denmark.   _____

Vocabulary in Context   **6**   In this passage, the word <u>currency</u> means
☐ a. exchange.
☐ b. money.
☐ c. expensive.
☐ d. cents.   _____

Add your scores for questions 1–6. Enter the total here and on the graph on page 158.   **Total Score**   _____

25 Why Equations Don't Have Answers

If you are like most people, your earliest experiences in mathematics were computing answers to arithmetic problems. Many students have difficulty when they first begin studying algebra because they have the belief that *all of* math is about determining answers. To understand why this is untrue, compare these mathematical problems:

What is 45×678? $\qquad\qquad$ $45 \times 678 = n$

The first problem is a question, and it has an answer: 30,510. The second problem is not a question; it is a statement in the form of an equation. To make this statement true, you need to find a number value for the letter n so that both sides of the equation are equal. Of course, the correct value is the same as the answer to the question "What is 45×678?"—30,510. This value, 30,510, is called the *solution* to the equation—the number that makes both sides of the equation equal.

Why is this distinction between answer and solution important for students to understand? Most equations are more complicated than $45 \times 678 = n$. In the more complicated equations, arriving at the solution requires performing a series of steps. To do this correctly, students learn they must "do the same thing" to both sides of an equation at each steps. Solving a complicated equation involves working through a series of equations till you end up with a simple equation like $n = 30,510$.

Many equations do not have a single number for a solution; instead, they have a whole set of numbers. In the equation $2a \times b = 12$, for example, one solution is to substitute 2 for a and 3 for b, but another is to substitute 1 and 6 (try it). And infinitely many more solutions exist. So "What is the answer to $2a \times b = 12$?" is a <u>meaningless</u> question. There is no answer to such an equation, only a set of solutions.

Main Idea	1		
		Answer	**Score**
Mark the *main idea*		M	15
Mark the statement that is *too broad*		B	5
Mark the statement that is *too narrow*		N	5

a. Some equations involve going through a whole series of steps.	☐	____
b. Arithmetic and algebra are different.	☐	____
c. Equations can't be "answered"; they must be "solved."	☐	____

Subject Matter   **2**   This passage is mainly about
  ☐ a. doing arithmetic accurately.
  ☐ b. why equations have solutions rather than answers.
  ☐ c. what *n* stands for in two different problems.
  ☐ d. solving difficult equations.   _____

Supporting Details   **3**   At each step in solving an equation, you must
  ☐ a. check that you have the right answer.
  ☐ b. show your solution on a graph.
  ☐ c. show your solution on a diagram
  ☐ d. do the same thing to both sides.   _____

Conclusion   **4**   The author has written this passage because
  ☐ a. some students find arithmetic confusing.
  ☐ b. some students find algebra confusing.
  ☐ c. some equations have many answers.
  ☐ d. all equations are quite complicated.   _____

Clarifying Devices   **5**   The passage explains the distinction between *answer* and *solution* by
  ☐ a. presenting a diagram.
  ☐ b. giving and explaining examples.
  ☐ c. showing the solution to a difficult equation.
  ☐ d. describing a graph.   _____

Vocabulary in Context   **6**   In this passage, the word <u>meaningless</u> means
  ☐ a. having several meanings.
  ☐ b. being very important.
  ☐ c. without meaning.
  ☐ d. meaning different things at different times.   _____

Add your scores for questions 1–6. Enter the total here and on the graph on page 158.   **Total Score**   _____

26 How Much Do You Save?

Stores often use sales to attract customers. A store might display a large sign such as Clearance Sale! Everything 30 Percent Off! To determine the savings on an article that is 30 percent off, you need to know how to do computations with percentages.

Most people recognize that 50 percent equals one-half and 25 percent equals one-fourth, but other percentages such as 30 percent or 45 percent may be mysteries. A percentage can be expressed as a fraction with the bottom number 100. Here are two examples using 50 percent and 25 percent. The reduced forms of the fractions show why 50 percent equals one-half and 25 percent equals one-fourth.

$$50 \text{ percent} = \frac{50}{100} = \frac{1}{2} \qquad 25 \text{ percent} = \frac{25}{100} = \frac{1}{4}$$

An essential concept that will assist you in computing percentages is that any fraction is a different way of writing division. The following examples show how percentages can be written as fractions and as division statements.

$$30 \text{ percent} = \frac{30}{100} = 30 \div 100 \qquad 45 \text{ percent} = \frac{45}{100} = 45 \div 100$$

To compute 30 percent of a price, perform these two steps: multiply by 30 and then divide by 100. This two-step strategy can help you solve any percentage problem. To prove to yourself that the strategy works, experiment with a problem such as 50 percent of $18. (You know before you start that the answer should be $9.) Using a calculator, multiply 50 times 18 to get 900; then divide 900 by 100 to get 9.

You probably won't <u>employ</u> this strategy with percentage problems that you can easily calculate on your own. But when you encounter more challenging percentage problems, the multiply-divide strategy will always work.

Main Idea	1	Answer	Score
	Mark the *main idea*	M	15
	Mark the statement that is *too broad*	B	5
	Mark the statement that is *too narrow*	N	5

a. Computing percentages is done by multiplying and then dividing by 100. ☐ _____

b. Computing percentages is difficult for many people. ☐ _____

c. A savings of 25 percent means that you save one-fourth of the regular price. ☐ _____

Subject Matter   **2**   Another good title for this passage would be
- [ ] a. Avoiding Trouble with Fractions.
- [ ] b. Comparing Prices on Sale Merchandise.
- [ ] c. Multiplying and Dividing.
- [ ] d. Finding a Percent of a Price.   _____

Supporting Details   **3**   A percentage can be expressed as
- [ ] a. a fraction with a top number of 100.
- [ ] b. a fraction with a bottom number of 100.
- [ ] c. always a very large number.
- [ ] d. a way of not getting cheated at a sale.   _____

Conclusion   **4**   To figure out 45 percent of $30,
- [ ] a. multiply 45 times 30 and divide the answer by 100.
- [ ] b. multiply 100 times 30 and divide the answer by 45.
- [ ] c. make $30 into a fraction.
- [ ] d. realize that 45 percent equals one-fourth.   _____

Clarifying Devices   **5**   The writer introduces this passage by
- [ ] a. discussing what 25 percent and 50 percent are equal to.
- [ ] b. telling what the word *percent* means.
- [ ] c. describing how percentages are used in sales.
- [ ] d. telling how percentages are calculated.   _____

Vocabulary in Context   **6**   In this passage, the word <u>employ</u> means to
- [ ] a. forget.
- [ ] b. hire.
- [ ] c. use.
- [ ] d. understand.   _____

Add your scores for questions 1–6. Enter the total here and on the graph on page 159.   **Total Score**   _____

27 Beyond the Domino

Dominoes is familiar game played with rectangular tiles. Each tile is made by joining two squares. Domino-like shapes can also be formed by joining more than two squares. Such geometric shapes are called *polyominoes.* The most popular polyominoes are the pentominoes, which are made by joining five squares. (*Pento-* means "five.") Below are the 12 possible pentominoes and one of the rectangles they can form.

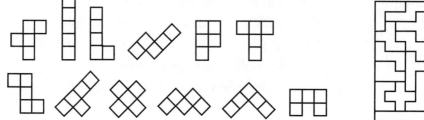

In a typical puzzle, you are given only the outline of the final shape. You build that shape using all 12 pieces, with no overlaps and no "holes."

Another kind of pentomino puzzle uses only 10 of the 12 pieces. For this puzzle, select any one piece. Then use 9 of the other pieces to "triplicate" the piece; that is, make a figure that has the same shape but triple the dimensions. The diagram to the right triplicates one of the pieces. Try to triplicate the other pieces.

Pentomino puzzles are a great way to improve your <u>visual</u> thinking skills. And they are lots of fun!

Main Idea   1

	Answer	Score
Mark the *main idea*	M	15
Mark the statement that is *too broad*	B	5
Mark the statement that is *too narrow*	N	5

a. A pentomino is made up of five squares. ☐ _____

b. Pentominoes are geometric shapes that can be used in visual puzzles. ☐ _____

c. Many people enjoy geometric puzzles. ☐ _____

Subject Matter **2** This passage is mainly about
- [ ] a. how to solve geometric puzzles.
- [ ] b. why geometric puzzles are popular.
- [ ] c. dominoes.
- [ ] d. pentominoes and pentomino puzzles.

_____

Supporting Details **3** A pentomino piece is made of
- [ ] a. 5 squares.
- [ ] b. 12 squares.
- [ ] c. 5 rectangles.
- [ ] d. 12 rectangles.

_____

Conclusion **4** You can conclude from this passage that
- [ ] a. you can make a complete square from pentomino pieces.
- [ ] b. rectangles can be of different lengths and widths.
- [ ] c. pentominoes can be bought in toy stores.
- [ ] d. pentominoes are a fairly new game.

_____

Clarifying Devices **5** The writer pictures the 12 pentominoes to
- [ ] a. help you see how many kinds there are.
- [ ] b. prove that they are easy to make.
- [ ] c. show that they are fun to play with.
- [ ] d. show that each one has four sides.

_____

Vocabulary in Context **6** In this passage, <u>visual</u> means having
- [ ] a. to do with hearing.
- [ ] b. to do with vision.
- [ ] c. many shapes.
- [ ] d. many sizes.

_____

Add your scores for questions 1–6. Enter the total here and on the graph on page 159. **Total Score** _____

28 Prime and Composite Numbers

One important way of classifying a whole number is by whether it is prime or composite. A prime number is a whole number greater than 1. It can have only two factors, or numbers that can be multiplied to produce it. These are the number itself and the number 1. The number 6 is not prime because it has the factors 2 and 3. If a number is not prime, like the example number 6, then it is composite—it is "composed" of its different factors.

To identify all prime numbers less than 100, start with a grid. Shade in all the multiples of two: 4, 6, and so on (as shown below). Shade in the multiples of 3, 5, and 7. The unshaded numbers are prime numbers.

You'll see from your diagram that a prime number greater than 2 has to end in the digit 1, 3, 7, or 9. But other than that, there apparently isn't any obvious pattern to the frequency of the primes. In fact, many renowned mathematicians have been fascinated with prime numbers, wondering if there *is* a complex pattern to their occurrence.

	2	3	4	5	6	7	8	9	10
11	12	13	14	15	16	17	18	19	20
21	22	23	24	25	26	27	28	29	30
31	32	33	34	35	36	37	38	39	40
41	412	43	44	45	46	47	48	49	50
51	52	53	54	55	56	57	58	59	60
61	62	63	64	65	66	67	68	69	70
71	72	73	74	75	76	77	78	79	80
81	82	83	84	85	86	87	88	89	90
91	92	93	94	95	96	97	98	99	100

Prime numbers have recently been put to an important use. Let's say a very large number, one with 120 digits, has only four factors: 1, itself, and two roughly equal prime numbers. (Those prime numbers might have 40 or 50 digits themselves.) Mathematicians believe that figuring out what those factors are can take years, even on the fastest computers. So these sorts of numbers are used in creating a procedure called *oblivious transfer,* a method of providing secure Internet transactions.

Main Idea   1

	Answer	Score
Mark the *main idea*	M	15
Mark the statement that is *too broad*	B	5
Mark the statement that is *too narrow*	N	5

a. The only even prime number is 2. ☐ _____

b. Prime numbers are part of mathematics. ☐ _____

c. Mathematicians consider prime numbers both interesting and useful. ☐ _____

Subject Matter   **2**   This passage is mainly concerned with
☐ a. prime numbers and their use.
☐ b. prime numbers between 1 and 200.
☐ c. whether there is a pattern in how often prime numbers occur.
☐ d. composite numbers and their use.   _____

Supporting Details   **3**   The number 6 is not a prime number because it
☐ a. is less than 100.
☐ b. is an even number.
☐ c. has other factors besides itself and 1.
☐ d. is not a whole number.   _____

Conclusion   **4**   This passage leads the reader to conclude that
☐ a. there are no prime numbers over 100.
☐ b. prime numbers can be very large.
☐ c. prime numbers cannot end in 3.
☐ d. mathematicians have identified every prime number that exists.   _____

Clarifying Devices   **5**   The diagram helps show that prime numbers
☐ a. are only even numbers.
☐ b. are greater than 2.
☐ c. require multiplication skills.
☐ d. have no obvious repeating pattern.   _____

Vocabulary in Context   **6**   In this passage, the word <u>secure</u> means
☐ a. unlikely.
☐ b. simple.
☐ c. safe.
☐ d. inexpensive.   _____

Add your scores for questions 1–6. Enter the total here and on the graph on page 159.   **Total Score**   _____

29 Random Numbers

What does the word *random* mean to you? You might think of events that are unpredictable. Or you might think of a series of numbers with no obvious pattern. Most people agree that tossing a coin results in a random outcome. Many have a false belief, though, that after a long sequence of heads the toss is more than 50 percent likely to be tails. Such a belief is known, for reasons you can imagine, as the "gambler's <u>fallacy</u>."

The need for random numbers or procedures occurs more often than you might think. In statistics, a sequence of outcomes or number choices is defined as random if each outcome is not influenced by the previous ones. So anyone who buys a ticket for a lottery wants to be sure that the results are truly random. And when doing such things as polling, statisticians need to pick random samples. This way, they ensure that their poll results will have validity. Computers are used to generate lists of random numbers for statistical and scientific work.

When might you need to use random numbers? People today use numbers in secret passwords for computer or banking access. Many people do not choose these numbers wisely. It is *not* a good idea, for example, to use part of your telephone number, social security number, or address. You could instead pick a number from a table of random numbers. But you might not have such a table handy. Consider this simpler, more practical way of getting a random number. Write the digits 0 through 9 on ten slips of paper. Then put them in a bag, and draw the needed number of digits. The key idea behind secret passwords is to use numbers that would be almost impossible for someone to guess.

Main Idea   1

	Answer	Score
Mark the *main idea*	M	15
Mark the statement that is *too broad*	B	5
Mark the statement that is *too narrow*	N	5

a. Random numbers are needed in many everyday transactions.	☐	____
b. Tossing a coin is a random procedure.	☐	____
c. Number patterns can be described in different ways.	☐	____

Score 15 points for each correct answer.   **Score**

Subject Matter   **2**   This passage is mainly about
- ☐ a. ways of winning at games of chance.
- ☐ b. setting up statistical experiments.
- ☐ c. remembering computer passwords.
- ☐ d. choosing and using random numbers.   _____

Supporting Details   **3**   If two events are random, then
- ☐ a. they are closely related.
- ☐ b. they occur at the same time.
- ☐ c. the second event does not depend on the first event.
- ☐ d. the events must involve large numbers.   _____

Conclusion   **4**   Random numbers must be selected
- ☐ a. from a hat.
- ☐ b. with a number pattern in mind.
- ☐ c. with no way to control or influence the choice.
- ☐ d. from a random number table.   _____

Clarifying Devices   **5**   In the final paragraph, the writer shows how random numbers
- ☐ a. can be used to pick passwords.
- ☐ b. are important in statistical work.
- ☐ c. are organized into tables.
- ☐ d. are composed of one-digit numerals.   _____

Vocabulary in Context   **6**   In this passage, the word <u>fallacy</u> means
- ☐ a. a lie.
- ☐ b. a mistaken belief.
- ☐ c. an argument.
- ☐ d. a choice.   _____

Add your scores for questions 1–6. Enter the total here and on the graph on page 159.   **Total Score**   _____

30 "Monday's Child Is Fair of Face"

When the Kaminsky sisters were children, their grandmother taught them a nursery rhyme. According to this rhyme, the day of the week you were born on determined your <u>dominant</u> character trait: "Monday's child is fair of face. Tuesday's child is full of grace," and so on. Victoria's older sister Alexandra used to brag about how "fair of face" she was because she had been born on a Monday. She asserted that Victoria's birth day was a Wednesday, and thus her sister was "full of woe." (Vicky vehemently denied this, although she wasn't absolutely certain what *woe* meant.) Their mom said she couldn't recall the days they were born on and she wished they would stop arguing.

When she was old enough to figure out the problem mathematically, Victoria set out to discover whether or not her birth date, November 26, 1954, had truly fallen on a Wednesday. She started with Pearl Harbor Day, December 7, 1941, because she knew it had been a Sunday. Victoria calculated that she had been born almost 13 years later $(1954 - 1941 = 13)$. She multiplied 13×365 days for a product of 4,745 days. Then she added 3 leap days (because 1944, 1948, and 1952 were leap years). Her total, 4,748, was the number of days between December 7, 1941 and December 7, 1954.

Victoria then subtracted 11 days (the number of days between November 26 and December 7) for a difference of 4,737. Next, she needed to calculate how many extra days beyond a week that was. Dividing 4,737 by 7, she got an answer of about 676 and $\frac{7}{10}$ weeks. That $\frac{7}{10}$ translated into 5 days. This meant that November 26, 1954, fell on a *Friday* (Sunday + 5 days)! Friday's child was "loving and giving."

She was even more pleased to discover that Alexandra's birthday, October 16, 1952, was actually a Thursday. Thursday's child, says the old rhyme, "has far to go."

Main Idea 1

	Answer	Score
Mark the *main idea*	M	15
Mark the statement that is *too broad*	B	5
Mark the statement that is *too narrow*	N	5

a. Vicky used math to prove her sister wrong. ☐ _____

b. Sisters often tease each other. ☐ _____

c. Victoria was born on a Friday, and Alexandra was born on a Thursday. ☐ _____

Subject Matter   **2**   Another good title for this passage might be

☐ a. Proving a Point with Math.

☐ b. Children's Nursery Rhymes.

☐ c. The Kaminsky Sisters.

☐ d. Pearl Harbor Day.   _____

Supporting Details   **3**   Victoria started her calculations with Pearl Harbor Day because

☐ a. it was her birthday.

☐ b. it was her sister's birthday.

☐ c. she knew it was on a Sunday.

☐ d. it occurred in 1941.   _____

Conclusion   **4**   We can conclude from reading the passage that

☐ a. Victoria did not get good grades in math.

☐ b. Victoria was 13 years old on Pearl Harbor Day.

☐ c. the sisters seldom argued.

☐ d. the sisters were competitive with each other.   _____

Clarifying Devices   **5**   This passage is developed mainly through

☐ a. giving examples to support a main idea.

☐ b. listing events in reverse time order.

☐ c. explaining the steps in a process.

☐ d. comparing and contrasting.   _____

Vocabulary in Context   **6**   In this passage, <u>dominant</u> means

☐ a. largest.

☐ b. least noticeable.

☐ c. most important or influential.

☐ d. loudest.   _____

Add your scores for questions 1–6. Enter the total here and on the graph on page 159.   **Total Score**   _____

31 Making a Budget

Making a budget can help people save for important purchases or just get their finances under control. Budgeting requires very little math, but it does mean keeping track of expenditures.

Start by selecting several large categories such as rent, <u>utilities</u>, telephone, food, and transportation. Then add a final category called "other" for the rest of your expenses. The categories you select will depend on how you spend your money. Next, pull out your checkbook and credit card statements. Use at least three months worth of numbers—six months is even better. When you add up what you've been spending for each category, the results may surprise you! You may not realize how much you spend on items such as clothing, eating out, and entertainment.

If you want a visual picture of your expenditures, you can use a circle graph. To create such a graph, you'll need a tool called a *protractor*, a device used to draw angles. As an example, let's say a person spent $4,325 in the last month. Of that amount, $725 went for rent. To draw the section on the graph for rent, divide the category amount ($725) by the total ($4,325). Then multiply by 360 degrees. You would get 60.3 degrees, the angle for the "rent" section on the graph.

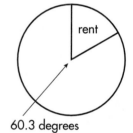

rent

60.3 degrees

Once you fully understand how you are spending your money, you can make better-informed decisions about financial matters. If you want to save for a big purchase, you can decide which categories you can trim down.

Main Idea	1		
		Answer	Score
	Mark the *main idea*	M	15
	Mark the statement that is *too broad*	B	5
	Mark the statement that is *too narrow*	N	5

a. When making a budget, it is best to break down spending into categories like food and rent. ☐ _____

b. Circle graphs are useful items. ☐ _____

c. Making a budget requires an understanding of past expenditures. ☐ _____

Subject Matter   2   This passage mostly focuses on
- ☐ a. the importance of using graphs.
- ☐ b. saving money for important purchases.
- ☐ c. an introduction to making a personal budget.
- ☐ d. using a protractor to draw angles. _____

Supporting Details   3   A protractor is a
- ☐ a. circle graph.
- ☐ b. budget.
- ☐ c. category of expenditures.
- ☐ d. tool for drawing angles. _____

Conclusion   4   A completed circle graph for a budget should show
- ☐ a. all the money that is spent over a month or other period.
- ☐ b. mainly amounts for food and transportation.
- ☐ c. the amount a person plans to make in the future.
- ☐ d. all rent increases for the past three years. _____

Clarifying Devices   5   The diagram of the circle graph in the passage is intended to show
- ☐ a. a completed sample budget.
- ☐ b. the categories to use in making a budget.
- ☐ c. a sample first step in figuring out spending.
- ☐ d. how to use a protractor. _____

Vocabulary in Context   6   In this passage, the word <u>utilities</u> means
- ☐ a. useful devices or machines.
- ☐ b. services such as electricity, gas, and water.
- ☐ c. computer programs for specific tasks.
- ☐ d. all large expenses. _____

Add your scores for questions 1–6. Enter the total here and on the graph on page 159.   Total Score _____

32 The Quadragenarian in the Quadrangle

If you know French or Spanish, you should have an easy time understanding words based on Latin or Greek number forms. The chart below <u>illustrates</u> this.

	1	2	3	4	5	6	7	8	9	10
French	un	deux	trois	quatre	cinq	six	sept	huit	neuf	dix
Spanish	uno	dos	tres	cuatro	cinco	seis	siete	ocho	nueve	diez
Latin	uni-	duo-	tri-	quadr-	quin-	sex-	sept-	oct-	novem-	decem-
Greek	mono-	di-	tri-	tetra-	penta-	hex-	hepta-	oct-	ennea-	deca-

Use the chart to help you read this paragraph. See that quadragenarian leading a quadruped through the quadrangle? In November he will have triple bypass surgery. He has completed his insurance forms in quintuplicate, but he still has a myriad of things to do before entering the hospital. Next year he hopes to enter a pentathlon; he has a monomania about sports that I find unique. His friends unite in the hope that a decade from now, when he is a quinquagenarian, he will slow down a little— they tell him that a century ago he wouldn't have lived this long.

Now read the numerical "translation." See that man between 40 and 49 leading a four-footed creature through the courtyard surrounded on four sides by buildings? In the ninth month of the year (according to an early Roman calendar), he will have heart surgery bypassing three of his arteries. He has completed five copies of his insurance forms, but he still has a great many things to do before entering the hospital (*myria* means "10,000" or "a great many" in Greek). Next year he hopes to enter an athletic competition involving five different events. He has a craziness that makes him focus on one topic—in this instance, sports. I think he is the only one who is this way. His friends are one in the hope that 10 years from now, when he is between 50 and 59, he will slow down a little. Had he lived 100 years ago, he wouldn't have lived this long.

Main Idea   1

	Answer	Score
Mark the *main idea*	M	15
Mark the statement that is *too broad*	B	5
Mark the statement that is *too narrow*	N	5

a. *Penta-* means "five" in Greek. ☐ _____

b. Greek and Latin number words can help you understand unfamiliar words. ☐ _____

c. Many words have foreign roots. ☐ _____

Subject Matter 2 Another good title for this passage might be
☐ a. Triple Bypass Surgery.
☐ b. Studying Greek and Latin.
☐ c. The History of Our Language.
☐ d. Greek and Latin Number Words. _____

Supporting 3 A quinquagenarian is someone
Details ☐ a. between 40 and 59.
☐ b. between 50 and 59.
☐ c. who is crazy about sports.
☐ d. who does a task five times. _____

Conclusion 4 After reading this passage, you can conclude that
☐ a. very few words are based on Latin or Greek.
☐ b. many words are based on Latin and Greek.
☐ c. to understand numbers, it's important to know French or Spanish.
☐ d. words with Latin or Greek roots are rarely useful in math. _____

Clarifying 5 In the final paragraph, the author puts quotation
Devices marks around *translation* to show that
☐ a. "translation" isn't exactly the right word for what follows.
☐ b. someone's exact words are being quoted.
☐ c. "translation" has a Greek root.
☐ d. you need to know Latin to understand what follows. _____

Vocabulary 6 In this passage, illustrates means
in Context ☐ a. draws a picture.
☐ b. helps write a book.
☐ c. makes clear.
☐ d. draws lines and boxes. _____

Add your scores for questions 1–6. Enter the total here **Total**
and on the graph on page 159. **Score** _____

33 Converting Measurements

Every once in a while, you may need to change a measurement from one unit to another. You might measure a window in inches and then need to find the number of yards of fabric for a curtain.

Unit conversion of this sort is based on a simple mathematics principle: Multiplying a number times 1 does not change its value. To use the principle in converting measurements, find the conversion factor; for example, 1 yard = 36 inches. Conversion factors can be found in dictionaries or encyclopedias. Write the conversion factor as a fraction, with 1 yard on the top and 36 inches on the bottom. This fraction equals the number 1 because, even though they are in different measures, the top and bottom quantities have the same value. If a window is 60 inches long, multiply 60 inches times the fraction to change the measurement to yards.

$$\frac{1 \text{ yard}}{36 \text{ inches}} \times 60 \text{ inches} = \frac{60}{36} \text{ (or } 60 \div 36) = 1\frac{2}{3} \text{ yards}$$

Here is a more complicated example that shows how to change 50 miles per hour into meters per second. Two fractions are used, one to convert the miles to meters and another to convert the hours to seconds.

$$\frac{50 \text{ miles}}{1 \text{ hour}} \times \frac{1609 \text{ m}}{1 \text{ mile}} \times \frac{1 \text{ hour}}{3600 \text{ sec}} = \frac{50 \times 1609}{3600} \text{ (or } 50 \times 1609 \div 3600) = 22.3 \text{ m/sec}$$

Notice that miles is on the *top* of the first fraction and on the *bottom* of the second fraction. Positioned in this way, the units cancel each other out. This second example may look complicated, but all you have done is multiply 50 miles per hour times the number 1 twice. You haven't <u>altered</u> the actual quantity, only the units in which it is named.

Main Idea	1		
		Answer	**Score**
	Mark the *main idea*	M	15
	Mark the statement that is *too broad*	B	5
	Mark the statement that is *too narrow*	N	5
	a. Unit conversions use math.	☐	____
	b. To convert a unit of measurement, multiply by an appropriate fraction.	☐	____
	c. To change inches to yards, divide the number of inches by 36.	☐	____

Subject Matter   **2**   This passage is mainly about
- ☐ a. multiplying and dividing.
- ☐ b. inches and yards.
- ☐ c. converting units of measurement.
- ☐ d. estimating with measurements.   _____

Supporting Details   **3**   A conversion fraction equals 1 because
- ☐ a. all fractions equal 1.
- ☐ b. the top and bottom quantities have the same value.
- ☐ c. the top and bottom numbers are the same.
- ☐ d. the two numbers are found in a dictionary.   _____

Conclusion   **4**   Understanding conversion factors can be useful
- ☐ a. in a job where you must change feet to meters.
- ☐ b. when buying running shoes.
- ☐ c. when weighing apples in a fruit market.
- ☐ d. in a job where you use computers.   _____

Clarifying Devices   **5**   The writer explains converting units of measurement by
- ☐ a. describing something that actually happened.
- ☐ b. defining _conversion._
- ☐ c. giving two mathematical examples.
- ☐ d. giving a history of this type of conversion.   _____

Vocabulary in Context   **6**   In this passage, the word <u>altered</u> means
- ☐ a. changed.
- ☐ b. prayed for.
- ☐ c. destroyed.
- ☐ d. measured.   _____

Add your scores for questions 1–6. Enter the total here and on the graph on page 159.   **Total Score**   _____

34 Storing a Million Dollars at Home

The only trouble with being rich these days is that you can't really interact with your riches. Novelist George Eliot wrote of a miser named Silas Marner who kept his loot concealed under his floor. Every night he had the pleasure of counting his fortune, basking in the glow of golden coins in candlelight. Today if you were a millionaire, you would probably bank your money or perhaps invest it in mutual funds or real estate. But if you *were* to store a million dollars at home, how much space would be involved?

Picture a shoebox about 5 inches wide, 12 inches long, and 5.5 inches tall. Now imagine your million is stored in quarter rolls (each roll, containing $10, is a cylinder about 2.75 inches long and an inch in diameter). You can easily fit four rows of four rolls into the bottom of your box, and you can stack the rolls four layers high (that's 64 rolls, or $640). Now visualize a small empty room in your home—a closed-in porch, perhaps—about nine feet square. Envision yourself laying down a layer of wall-to-wall shoeboxes (each box is weighty since it's chock-full of quarter rolls); the layer is 21 boxes wide and eight boxes long, for a total of 168 boxes.

After stacking up 9 layers of quarter-filled boxes, you've constructed a rectangular solid about 49.5 inches tall (about chest high). Absolutely exhausted, you sit down to compute the amount you've stacked so far. Nine layers of 168 = 1,512 boxes. Since each box contains $640, you've already stacked up $967,680! The amount you have yet to stack, $32,320, means that you have 50.5 boxes of $640 to go. Crawling on hands and knees atop your <u>edifice</u>, you lay down 50 more boxes, thereby accounting for $32,000. There is still $320 remaining from your million to stack. You pile on 32 quarter rolls from your last shoebox—two layers of 16 rolls. Your porch is out of commission, but you've got your million at home where you can gloat over it!

Main Idea	1		
		Answer	**Score**
	Mark the *main idea*	M	15
	Mark the statement that is *too broad*	B	5
	Mark the statement that is *too narrow*	N	5
	a. In quarter rolls, $640 fills one shoebox.	☐	_____
	b. Some people store money at home.	☐	_____
	c. You can visualize $1,000,000 by figuring out how much space it fills.	☐	_____

Score 15 points for each correct answer.   Score

Subject Matter   2   Another good title for this passage would be
         ☐ a. Counting by Candlelight.
         ☐ b. Visualizing a Fortune.
         ☐ c. Putting Quarters in Shoeboxes.
         ☐ d. Multiplying and Dividing.   _____

Supporting   3   The money storage described in this passage
Details   is done by putting
         ☐ a. 9 layers of quarter rolls in each shoebox.
         ☐ b. 640 quarter rolls in each shoebox.
         ☐ c. $64 in each shoebox.
         ☐ d. 64 quarter rolls in each shoebox.   _____

Conclusion   4   The author wants readers to conclude that
         ☐ a. it is unsafe to invest in real estate.
         ☐ b. Silas Marner was a dishonest person.
         ☐ c. it is fun to imagine keeping $1,000,000
            at home, but it is not a practical idea.
         ☐ d. you can keep a lot of money at home if
            you are willing to work hard at storing it.   _____

Clarifying   5   The idea of quarter rolls in shoeboxes helps
Devices   readers to
         ☐ a. picture a large amount of money.
         ☐ b. recall the main character in *Silas Marner*.
         ☐ c. review multiplication and division skills.
         ☐ d. figure out why banks do not store coins.   _____

Vocabulary   6   The word <u>edifice</u> means
in Context
         ☐ a. structure.
         ☐ b. room.
         ☐ c. sculpture.
         ☐ d. lesson.   _____

Add your scores for questions 1–6. Enter the total here   Total
and on the graph on page 159.   Score   _____

35 Patching Things Up with Your Bank

Reconciliation can refer to the act of patching up a lovers' quarrel; similarly, when you reconcile your checkbook, you and your bank hash out "misunderstandings." Suppose Akira Horikoshi's checking account register for the new year begins like this:

NUMBER	DATE	DESCRIPTION OF TRANSACTION	PAYMENT/DEBIT (-)	✓ T	FEE IF ANY (-)	DEPOSIT/CREDIT (+)	BALANCE $ 6,000 00
90	1/2	John Scandellari (landlord)	$700.00	$		$	5,300 00
91	1/5	Health Conscious Insurance	130.00				5170 00

On January 7, Akira deposits $1,000 and writes a check for $60; on 1/8, he writes a check for $80; on 1/9, he writes a check for $50. A little adding and subtracting shows that his balance is now $5,980. Aki keeps <u>meticulous</u> track of his account, dutifully subtracting the amount of each check right after he writes it, but then he suddenly gets a baffling bank statement saying he has $5,150, almost $1,000 less than he thought.

If such a discrepancy has ever occurred with your bank statement, you might follow Akira's procedure to reconcile it. First, he noted that the statement says "covers transactions through January 6"—so one reason he and his bank "disagree" is that this statement doesn't account for anything that happened after that date. All it covers is the initial $6,000 deposit, the first two checks he wrote (for $700 and $130), and a pair of items he'd forgotten: a $10 monthly checking fee and a $10 check printing charge.

Subtracting these two items from his $5,980 balance gave Aki $5,960. He then totaled out any transactions occurring after January 6. The three checks he wrote add up to $190; subtracted from his 1/7 deposit of $1,000, this leaves $810—the exact difference between the $5,960 he believes he has and the $5,150 the bank said he has.

Main Idea   **1**

	Answer	Score
Mark the *main idea*	M	15
Mark the statement that is *too broad*	B	5
Mark the statement that is *too narrow*	N	5

a. It is fairly simple to balance a checking account. ☐ _____

b. Many people write checks. ☐ _____

c. Subtract the amount of each check after you write it. ☐ _____

Score 15 points for each correct answer.   **Score**

Subject Matter   **2**   This passage is mainly about
    ☐ a. writing checks to pay bills.
    ☐ b. patching up lovers' quarrels.
    ☐ c. balancing a checking account.
    ☐ d. thinking like a bank manager.   _____

Supporting   **3**   Akira began the new year with an opening
Details   balance of
    ☐ a. $1,000.
    ☐ b. $5,150.
    ☐ c. $5,940.
    ☐ d. $6,000.   _____

Conclusion   **4**   An important thing to figure out in balancing
    a checkbook is
    ☐ a. which checks have and have not cleared.
    ☐ b. how many checks you write every month.
    ☐ c. how many deposits you make in a year.
    ☐ d. how many deposits are more than $1,000.   _____

Clarifying   **5**   The two meanings for *reconciliation* suggest a
Devices   connection between balancing a checking account
    and
    ☐ a. opening a savings account.
    ☐ b. patching up a lovers' quarrel.
    ☐ c. adding several outstanding checks.
    ☐ d. juggling a career and a love life.   _____

Vocabulary   **6**   <u>Meticulous</u> means extremely
in Context
    ☐ a. sloppy.
    ☐ b. difficult.
    ☐ c. careful.
    ☐ d. metallic.   _____

Add your scores for questions 1–6. Enter the total here   **Total**
and on the graph on page 159.   **Score**   _____

36 Playing Havoc with Generations

In 1999 Daniel Benjamin noticed his university professor chatting with an elderly gentleman. The professor presently introduced Harrison Ruffin Tyler, a descendant of the 10th U.S. president, John Tyler. Since John Tyler was born in 1790 (as a child, he had met George Washington), Daniel speculated that Harrison was President Tyler's great-great-grandson. Daniel assumed that a generation is about 30 years long. He figured that if President Tyler had had a child when he was 30, that child (let's call him John 2) would have been born in 1820; if John 2 had had a child when *he* was 30, John 3, the president's grandson, would have been born in 1850. John 4, President Tyler's great-grandson, would have been born in 1880, and John 5, his great-great-grandson, would have come along in 1910.

Was Harrison Tyler "John 5"? To Daniel, Harrison looked about 65—not old enough to have been born in 1910. Daniel decided that Harrison might even be "John 6," the President's great-great-great-grandson. Imagine his surprise when Harrison Tyler began to speak of his *grandfather,* President John Tyler! Here's how this strange fluke occurred: after President Tyler's first wife, Letitia, died in 1842, he married a woman 30 years his junior, Julia Gardiner. In 1853 (when John was 63 years old) he and Julia had a son named Lyon Gardiner Tyler. Lyon, too, married twice. His second wife, Sue Ruffin, was 36 years younger than her husband. Lyon and Sue's son Harrison Ruffin Tyler was born in 1928, when Lyon was 75! Harrison was 71 in 1999.

So much time had <u>elapsed</u> between the births of John and Lyon and between the births of Lyon and Harrison that Harrison ended up way out of line with his family's generations. For example, Harrison's first cousin Robert Tyler Jones was 85 years older than Harrison—old enough to be Harrison's great-grandfather!

Main Idea	1		
		Answer	Score
	Mark the *main idea*	M	15
	Mark the statement that is *too broad*	B	5
	Mark the statement that is *too narrow*	N	5

		Answer	Score
a.	A generation can be short or long.	☐	____
b.	In Harrison Tyler's family, generations were unusually long.	☐	____
c.	Lyon Tyler was 75 when his son was born.	☐	____

Score 15 points for each correct answer.   **Score**

Subject Matter   **2**   This passage is mainly about
- ☐ a. John Tyler's presidency.
- ☐ b. second marriages to younger women.
- ☐ c. the unusual generations in Harrison Tyler's family.
- ☐ d. Harrison Tyler's affection for his late grandfather.

                _____

Supporting Details   **3**   Lyon Gardiner Tyler was born
- ☐ a. in 1842.
- ☐ b. when his father was 63.
- ☐ c. when his father was 30.
- ☐ d. in 1928.

                _____

Conclusion   **4**   Daniel made an error when he decided
- ☐ a. to subtract 1853 from 1928.
- ☐ b. that a generation must be 30 years.
- ☐ c. that John Tyler was older than Julia.
- ☐ d. to subtract 1790 from 1853.

                _____

Clarifying Devices   **5**   The names "John 2," "John 3," and so on, stand for
- ☐ a. Harrison Tyler's first cousins.
- ☐ b. John Tyler's many sons.
- ☐ c. generations of the Tyler family.
- ☐ d. actual individuals that Daniel had read about.

                _____

Vocabulary in Context   **6**   The word <u>elapsed</u> means
- ☐ a. collapsed.
- ☐ b. passed.
- ☐ c. argued.
- ☐ d. exclaimed.

                _____

Add your scores for questions 1–6. Enter the total here and on the graph on page 159.   **Total Score**   _____

37 If This Is San Francisco, It Must Be Yesterday

Tony Montecito is a U.S. citizen residing in Tokyo. On Friday, March 3, he attends an important business conference that lasts until noon. The next day, Saturday, March 4, Tony's brother is to be married in San Francisco, and Tony is best man. There will be a rehearsal banquet at 6 P.M. on Friday evening. Though a nonstop flight from Tokyo to San Francisco takes about nine hours, Tony arrives in plenty of time to take a siesta and a <u>leisurely</u> shower before Friday's rehearsal dinner.

Here is how this works. Suppose you live in California and your parents reside in Hawaii. Because it is two hours earlier in Hawaii than in California, your parents avoid calling too late in the evening; 9 P.M. in Hawaii is 11 P.M. in California. However, if your folks live in Tokyo and you call them at 9 in the evening on Saturday, California time, it will be 1 P.M. *Sunday* Tokyo time. The culprit is an imaginary north-south line called the International Dateline (IDL). It lies in the Pacific between Hawaii and Japan. If you cross the IDL traveling west, the time is 24 hours ahead. That is, if you approach the IDL at noon on Saturday, it will be Sunday noon as soon as you cross it. If you count the time zones between California and Tokyo, there are only seven. But you have to take that extra 24-hour day into account. Subtracting 7 hours from 24 hours gives you 17 hours, the difference between Tokyo and California time.

So Tony, his conference completed, departs from Tokyo at 4:30 P.M. on Friday. He is heading east. When he arrives in San Francisco after the nine-hour flight, it is 1:30 A.M. Saturday Tokyo time, but it is 8:30 A.M. *Friday* San Francisco time—or 17 hours earlier. Just as his plane crossed the IDL sometime Friday night, the time turned back 24 hours. It became Thursday night at the same time. That's why it's only Friday morning when he lands in San Francisco—Tony gets a second Friday free!

Main Idea	1		
		Answer	**Score**
	Mark the *main idea*	M	15
	Mark the statement that is *too broad*	B	5
	Mark the statement that is *too narrow*	N	5

a. The world has many time zones. ☐ _____

b. A traveler gains or loses a day crossing the International Date Line. ☐ _____

c. Tony left Tokyo at 4:30 P.M. Friday. ☐

Score 15 points for each correct answer.   Score

Subject Matter   **2**   Another good title for this passage would be
       ☐ a. With Time to Spare.
       ☐ b. A Family Wedding.
       ☐ c. Business Conference in Japan.
       ☐ d. In the Nick of Time.   _____

Supporting   **3**   It is 17 hours earlier in
Details
       ☐ a. New York than it is in California.
       ☐ b. Hawaii than it is in San Francisco.
       ☐ c. San Francisco than it is in Tokyo.
       ☐ d. Tokyo than it is in San Francisco.   _____

Conclusion   **4**   When traveling across the Pacific, one needs to
       ☐ a. plan on a 17-hour flight.
       ☐ b. fly from San Francisco to Hawaii to Tokyo.
       ☐ c. figure the IDL into one's schedule.
       ☐ d. try to avoid crossing the IDL.   _____

Clarifying   **5**   The story about Tony is told
Devices
       ☐ a. because it is true.
       ☐ b. as an example of how the IDL affects time.
       ☐ c. to show that weddings require careful
           planning.
       ☐ d. to interest the reader in how the wedding
           turns out.   _____

Vocabulary   **6**   The word <u>leisurely</u> means
in Context
       ☐ a. frantic.
       ☐ b. quick.
       ☐ c. warm.
       ☐ d. unhurried.   _____

Add your scores for questions 1–6. Enter the total here   **Total**
and on the graph on page 159.   **Score**   _____

38 Working Through a Math Puzzle

If you are as <u>intrigued</u> by mathematical games and puzzles as Veronica Tervalon is, proceed through the steps below with Veronica and see how this puzzle works.

On Halloween afternoon, 1999, this forwarded e-mail message appeared on Veronica's computer:

Dearest Friends and Esteemed Colleagues—We sincerely hope you'll enjoy this intriguing little mathematical game, which we assure you is anything but time-consuming: it takes approximately 30 seconds to complete. However, don't delay—the formula it is based on will be invalid when the new millennium commences.

(1) Pick the number of evenings per week that you would prefer dining in restaurants. [Veronica, who usually preferred her husband's cooking, chose 1.]

(2) Multiply your number by 2, and add 5. [Veronica's total was 7.]

(3) Multiply that total by 50. [Veronica's product was 350.]

(4) If you have already celebrated your birthday this year, add 1749; however, if your birthday is still to come, add 1748. [Since Veronica's birthday fell on December 31, she added 1748 for a sum of 2098.]

(5) Now subtract the four-digit number representing the year of your birth. [Veronica subtracted 1964 for a difference of 134.]

(6) These computations should have resulted in a three-digit number. The digit in the hundreds column should be your original number (number of evenings per week that you'd prefer dining in restaurants). [Yes, Veronica's number was 1.] *The other two digits should be your age.* [YES, Veronica was 34 years old!]

If an acquaintance of yours is a sophisticated mathematician who can create puzzles with numbers that automatically cancel themselves out, see if that person can adapt the data in this puzzle to make it work in the new millennium.

Main Idea	1		
		Answer	**Score**
	Mark the *main idea*	M	15
	Mark the statement that is *too broad*	B	5
	Mark the statement that is *too narrow*	N	5

a. A well-designed math puzzle will come up with the results it promises. ☐ ____

b. Math puzzles are very interesting. ☐ ____

c. Veronica worked the puzzle using her own numbers. ☐ ____

Score 15 points for each correct answer. **Score**

Subject Matter **2** Another good title for this passage might be
- [ ] a. Getting E-mail Messages.
- [ ] b. Halloween 1999.
- [ ] c. Creating a Brain Teaser.
- [ ] d. Solve Before the Millennium! _____

Supporting Details **3** Veronica was to add the number 1748
- [ ] a. if she hadn't yet had a birthday in 1999.
- [ ] b. if she had already had her birthday in 1999.
- [ ] c. to the number of evenings she preferred dining in restaurants.
- [ ] d. to her age. _____

Conclusion **4** A reason that your own numbers might not work in this puzzle is that
- [ ] a. it is no longer 1999.
- [ ] b. your birthday has already occurred this year.
- [ ] c. the steps are not in correct order.
- [ ] d. your numbers are probably the same as Veronica's. _____

Clarifying Devices **5** The writer uses italic type to
- [ ] a. show Veronica's calculations as she worked the puzzle.
- [ ] b. highlight the steps of the puzzle.
- [ ] c. show that certain words are important.
- [ ] d. convey how excited Veronica felt when the puzzle worked. _____

Vocabulary in Context **6** In this passage, <u>intrigued</u> means
- [ ] a. surprised.
- [ ] b. frightened.
- [ ] c. fascinated.
- [ ] d. bored. _____

Add your scores for questions 1–6. Enter the total here and on the graph on page 159. **Total Score** _____

39 Happy 22nd Birthday, Great-Great-Uncle Mike!

It is February 29, 2088, and Mike Slutzker is celebrating his 22nd birthday. His sister Shellby has come to attend the festivities; so have Shellby's children, grandchildren, great-grandchildren, and great-great-grandchildren. One of these great-great-grandchildren is Mike's 30-year-old great-great-niece. How, you might ask, is this possible?

The answer is that little Mikey Slutzker was born on February 29, 2000, a leap-year day. The following year, 2001, had no February 29, so Mikey's family decided to celebrate his birthday on February 28. But in 2004, when Mikey turned four, it was leap year again, and there was a February 29. His parents joked that Mikey was only one year old, since this was the first time since he was born that his actual birthday had come around again. After that, it became a family tradition to celebrate Mike's "fake birthdays" on February 28 of nonleap years and his "real birthdays" on February 29 of leap years and to pretend that he aged only one year for every four. Since 88 divided by 4 is 22, in 2088, a leap year, the family celebrated Mike's "real" 22nd birthday as well as his "fake" (his actual) 88th birthday.

The reason leap years exist is that ever since people began creating calendars, they were <u>plagued</u> by the difficulty of precisely calculating the length of a year. Calendar makers finally determined that a year is 365 days long, plus about 6 hours ($\frac{1}{4}$ of a day). If the calendar establishes a year that lasts 365 days when it actually lasts 365.25, after four years the calendar will be out of synch with the earth's orbit by a day. To correct the error, we have a leap year, or 366-day year, every four years.

Leap years are years that are exactly divisible by 4; for example, 1996 was a leap year, as was 1992. However, century years are exceptions to this rule. They are leap years only if they are exactly divisible by 400, such as 1600 and 2000.

Main Idea	1		
		Answer	**Score**
Mark the *main idea*		M	15
Mark the statement that is *too broad*		B	5
Mark the statement that is *too narrow*		N	5

a. Leap years were created because a year is a little longer than 365 days. ☐ _____

b. Mike was born on a leap-year day. ☐ _____

c. Calendars need to be accurate. ☐ _____

Subject Matter   **2**   The passage is primarily about
☐ a. Mike Slutzker and his family.
☐ b. leap years.
☐ c. calendars.
☐ d. birthday celebrations.   _____

Supporting   **3**   In 2088, Mike was actually
Details
☐ a. 22 years old.
☐ b. 30 years old.
☐ c. 88 years old.
☐ d. 4 years old.   _____

Conclusion   **4**   We can conclude from reading the passage that
☐ a. 2400 will be a leap year.
☐ b. 2058 will be a leap year.
☐ c. 2100 will be a leap year.
☐ d. 1200 was not a leap year.   _____

Clarifying   **5**   The story of Mike's "real" and "fake" birthdays
Devices   is presented to demonstrate
☐ a. a bizarre fact about Mike's family.
☐ b. how often leap years occur.
☐ c. that 88 divided by 22 is 4.
☐ d. the silliness of Michael's parents.   _____

Vocabulary   **6**   The word <u>plagued</u> means
in Context
☐ a. altered.
☐ b. assisted.
☐ c. brutalized.
☐ d. bothered.   _____

Add your scores for questions 1–6. Enter the total here   **Total**
and on the graph on page 159.   **Score**   _____

40 Riding the Stock Market Roller Coaster

Ileana Ionesco invested some of her savings in 1,000 shares of a company called Phosphorescent. In the table below, the columns labeled **High** and **Low** record the extremes of the daily fluctuations for each share of Fosphorescent stock; **Close** represents the trading price when the stock exchange stopped trading each afternoon. **Net Change** shows each day's gain or loss compared with the closing price on the previous trading day.

Date	High	Low	Close	Net Change
Mon 9/27	19.44	19.19	19.31	+ 0.13
Tues 9/28	19.88	19.13	19.38	+ 0.07
Wed 9/29	18.56	18.31	18.31	- 1.07
Thur 9/30	17.88	17.38	17.75	- 0.56
Fri 10/1	17.88	16.88	17.13	- 0.62

For example, on Wednesday the price of a share reached a high of $18.56. But when the market's final bell rang that day, the stock was selling for $18.31, which was its low for the day. This was $1.07 below Tuesday's closing price.

Even though some of the numbers in the Net Change column may seem miniscule, changes in the total value of Ileana's 1,000 shares can be substantial. The total value of Ileana's stocks at Tuesday's close was $19.38 × 1,000, or $19,380. However, by the end of the day on Wednesday, the total value had lost $1.07 × 1,000, or $1,070, so Ileana's stock was worth only $18,310. The most important thing to remember about the stock market is that it is unpredictable.

Imagine that on Monday, October 4, Forphorescent's president announces an upcoming merger and the share price skyrockets to a new annual high of $21.75. That overnight gain of $4.62 per share would increase Ileana's holdings by $4,620!

Main Idea   1

	Answer	Score
Mark the *main idea*	M	15
Mark the statement that is *too broad*	B	5
Mark the statement that is *too narrow*	N	5

a. Many people buy stock. ☐ _____

b. Illeana has stock in Fosphorescent. ☐ _____

c. Understanding stock tables can help you see how a stock's value changes. ☐ _____

Subject Matter	**2**	This passage's main purpose is to teach readers
		☐ a. that it is unwise to purchase stock.
		☐ b. how to divide using a calculator.
		☐ c. about stock market crashes.
		☐ d. how to read stock tables. _____

Supporting Details	**3**	The closing price of Fosphorescent on Tuesday, 9/28 was
		☐ a. $19.88.
		☐ b. $19.13.
		☐ c. $19.38.
		☐ d. $0.07. _____

Conclusion	**4**	The best day to sell Fosphorescent would have been
		☐ a. Friday, 10/1.
		☐ b. Thursday, 9/30.
		☐ c. Wednesday, 9/29.
		☐ d. Tuesday, 9/28. _____

Clarifying Devices	**5**	The table in this passage is useful for
		☐ a. finding the price of Fosphorescent stock at exactly noon on 9/27.
		☐ b. getting an overview of what the stock did in one week.
		☐ c. figuring out how much Illeana has earned so far in dividends.
		☐ d. learning Fosphorescent's price on Thursday, 9/23. _____

Vocabulary in Context	**6**	Minuscule means
		☐ a. tiny.
		☐ b. moderate.
		☐ c. unpredictable.
		☐ d. crablike. _____

Add your scores for questions 1–6. Enter the total here and on the graph on page 159.   **Total Score** _____

41 The Binary Number System

Looking at the numeral 1111111, you probably assume it has a value of one million, one hundred eleven thousand, one hundred eleven. But in the binary number system, the one used in computers, 1111111 represents a value of 127.

The decimal system—the system most commonly used today—got its name from the Latin word *decem,* which means "ten." In this system, every position in a number is the result of multiplying by 10. For example, there is a ones place, a tens place (1 × 10), a hundreds place (10 × 10), a thousands place (10 × 10 × 10), and so on. In the decimal system, the 1 on the far right of 1111111 represents 1, the 1 to the left of that represents 10, the 1 to the left of *that* represents 100, and so on.

In the binary system (*bi-* means "two" in Latin), every position in a number is the result of multiplying by 2. Like the decimal system, the binary system begins with a ones place; however, the place to the left of the ones place is the twos place (1 × 2), the place to the left of that is the fours place (2 × 2), the place to its left is the eights place (2 × 2 × 2), and so on. By adding all numbers in the top row of this diagram that represent 1's in the bottom row, you could figure out what 1111111 "translates" to.

64	32	16	8	4	2	1
1	1	1	1	1	1	1

Binary 1111111 is decimal 127; it equals 64 + 32 + 16 + 8 + 4 + 2 + 1.

Though binary numbers can be <u>entertaining</u> to look at, they are difficult for the average person to work with. Because only two digits are used, numbers quickly become very lengthy: if 100110011 in binary is only 407 in decimals, can you imagine how many digits are needed to "translate" a decimal number like 10,000? And adding or dividing such numbers is complicated indeed—a task best left to a computer!

Main Idea   1 ─────────────────────────────────────

	Answer	Score
Mark the *main idea*	M	15
Mark the statement that is *too broad*	B	5
Mark the statement that is *too narrow*	N	5

a. There are several number systems. ☐ ____

b. The binary number system is best used in computers. ☐ ____

c. The binary number 1111111 represents decimal 127. ☐ ____

Subject Matter   2   This passage is mostly about
- ☐ a. how the decimal system works.
- ☐ b. adding and dividing large numbers.
- ☐ c. how the binary system works.
- ☐ d. how computers are programmed.   _____

Supporting Details   3   The binary system first has a ones place and then a
- ☐ a. tens place, a hundreds place, and so on.
- ☐ b. hundreds place, a tens place, and so on.
- ☐ c. twos place, a threes place, and so on.
- ☐ d. twos place, a fours place, and so on.   _____

Conclusion   4   We can conclude from reading the passage that the binary system uses the digits
- ☐ a. 1 through 9.
- ☐ b. 0 through 9.
- ☐ c. 0, 1, and 2.
- ☐ d. 0 and 1.   _____

Clarifying Devices   5   The second and third paragraphs are developed mainly through
- ☐ a. listing events in time order.
- ☐ b. relating an anecdote.
- ☐ c. giving reasons to prove a point.
- ☐ d. showing similarities and differences.   _____

Vocabulary in Context   6   In this passage, <u>entertaining</u> means
- ☐ a. fun or amusing.
- ☐ b. serving food and drink to guests.
- ☐ c. complicated.
- ☐ d. singing and dancing.   _____

Add your scores for questions 1–6. Enter the total here and on the graph on page 159.   **Total Score**   _____

42 Buying and Maintaining an Economy Car

If you've ever been curious about how much it actually costs to own and operate a car, the following story demonstrates a way to figure out these expenses.

In 1994 Kimberly Ridgemont bought an economy car known as a Hedgehog. The total price, including sales tax and license, was $8,856.92. Kimberly paid $1,000 down and borrowed the rest, $7,856.92, from the National Automobile Corporation, the manufacturer of the Hedgehog, at an annual interest rate of 7.25 percent. Kim bought the car on July 31, 1994, and on September 1, her first payment of $156.50 was due. When she finished paying for the car in 1999, she wondered what her total purchase price actually came to. Since it had taken her 60 months to repay the loan, the total she had spent to purchase the car was $10,390 ($156.50 × 60 months + $1,000 down payment). Her calculations showed that she had paid, in addition to the purchase price, $1,533.08 in interest.

Soon after that, Kimberly decided to sell her Hedgehog and wanted to see how much the car had cost her per month. During the five years it had taken to pay off the loan, she had paid about $70 per month for car insurance, or $4,200 total. She had also spent about $30 per month for gas, for a total of $1,800, and about $380 per year in maintenance ($1,900 total). Adding these numbers to her total purchase cost of $10,390, Kimberly found that she had spent about $18,290 on her Hedgehog. Those were her expenses—but she also had made money on the car when she sold it for $3,640. Subtracting $3,640 from $18,290 lowered her expenses to $14,650. Dividing that number by 60 months, Kimberly calculated that her Hedgehog had cost her about $244.17 per month.

Main Idea	1	Answer	Score
	Mark the *main idea*	M	15
	Mark the statement that is *too broad*	B	5
	Mark the statement that is *too narrow*	N	5
	a. Kimberly got a car loan at 7.25 percent.	☐	____
	b. To figure total car costs, interest and maintenance expenses must be included.	☐	____
	c. Some cars can be bought and run cheaply.	☐	____

Score 15 points for each correct answer.   Score

Subject Matter   **2**   Another good title for this passage might be
- [ ] a. What Does It Cost to Own a Hedgehog?
- [ ] b. The Magnificent Hedgehog.
- [ ] c. Buying on Credit.
- [ ] d. Getting a Good Used Car.   _____

Supporting   **3**   Kimberly's total purchase price for the car was
Details
- [ ] a. $7,856.92.
- [ ] b. $10,390.
- [ ] c. $3,640.
- [ ] d. $1,533.08.   _____

Conclusion   **4**   Kimberly paid a total of $1,900 in maintenance
because
- [ ] a. she paid $380 a year for five years.
- [ ] b. she paid $380 a month for 60 months.
- [ ] c. the interest rate on her loan was
7.25 percent.
- [ ] d. she had a down payment of $1,000.   _____

Clarifying   **5**   The writer tells the story of Kimberly to
Devices
- [ ] a. show how frugal young women can be.
- [ ] b. present an example that sounds like real life.
- [ ] c. make you wonder what her next car will be.
- [ ] d. make you want to get as good an interest
rate as she did.   _____

Vocabulary   **6**   In this passage, <u>down</u> means
in Context
- [ ] a. in cash at the time of purchase.
- [ ] b. below.
- [ ] c. sad or unhappy.
- [ ] d. soft feathers or hair.   _____

Add your scores for questions 1–6. Enter the total here   Total
and on the graph on page 159.   Score   _____

43 Adding 100 Numbers in Minutes

As an adult, Carl Friedrich Gauss became a renowned mathematician, but as a young student in the Duchy of Brunswick (now a region of Germany), no one was yet aware of his amazing facility for discerning mathematical patterns. Apparently Carl (like many precocious children) was difficult for his teachers to control. One legend claims that, perhaps hoping to distract him for a time, a teacher ordered him to sit silently and add the numbers from 1 to 100. The teacher probably assumed that Carl would be challenged for hours, but minutes later the boy had the correct response.

Carl did what most trained mathematicians would have done: look for a pattern. Recently, Annabelle Leigh, an adult student of average mathematical aptitude, reasoned this way: If you add the numbers from 1 to 10, you get 55. If you add the numbers from 11 to 20, you get 155; the numbers from 21 to 30 total up to 255. Following this pattern, Annabelle added 55 + 155 + 255 + 355 + 455 + 555 + 655 + 755 + 855 + 955 = 5050. Annabelle determined the solution in about 15 minutes, but she was using a calculator. The young Carl Friedrich, who grew up in the late 1700s, obviously did not have access to this tool. Carl calculated his amazingly quick response by identifying this pattern:

1	2	3	4	5	6	7	8	9	and so on to 50
100	99	98	97	96	95	94	93	92	and so on to 51
101	101	101	101	101	101	101	101	101	and so on.

Once Carl had determined that the sum of each number pair is 101, all he needed to do was multiply 101 by 50, the number of addition problems needed to total up all the numbers, to arrive at the answer, 5050. Throughout his lifetime, Gauss created many more complex mathematical formulas, but perhaps no formula was quite as rewarding as this early challenge.

Main Idea	1		
		Answer	**Score**
	Mark the *main idea*	M	15
	Mark the statement that is *too broad*	B	5
	Mark the statement that is *too narrow*	N	5
	a. Gauss was a brilliant mathematician.	☐	____
	b. Young Carl used 50 × 101 = 5050.	☐	____
	c. Carl Gauss showed his talent by quickly solving a difficult problem.	☐	____

Subject Matter   2   Another good title for this passage might be
- [ ] a. A Simple, Brilliant Solution.
- [ ] b. Practice Makes Perfect.
- [ ] c. The Duchy of Brunswick.
- [ ] d. School Days in the 1700s.   _____

Supporting Details   3   Carl's solution involved
- [ ] a. adding multiples of 10 (10, 20, 30, etc.).
- [ ] b. working out a pattern.
- [ ] c. adding the numbers from 1 to 10, 11 to 20, and so on.
- [ ] d. adding $1 + 2 + 3 + 4$, and so on.   _____

Conclusion   4   We can conclude from the passage that
- [ ] a. some people are born with an extremely high level of mathematical aptitude.
- [ ] b. Carl had been studying math since age two.
- [ ] c. most bright kids can reason as well as Carl.
- [ ] d. the teacher disapproved of Carl's solution.   _____

Clarifying Devices   5   Annabelle Leigh's solution is mentioned to show
- [ ] a. how a present-day adult with a calculator might solve the problem.
- [ ] b. that women are just as smart as young boys.
- [ ] c. that calculators make all math easy.
- [ ] d. that some problems have several answers.   _____

Vocabulary in Context   6   The word <u>precocious</u> means
- [ ] a. adorable.
- [ ] b. developed earlier than usual.
- [ ] c. ill-mannered.
- [ ] d. slow to adapt to strict rules.   _____

Add your scores for questions 1–6. Enter the total here and on the graph on page 159.   Total Score   _____

44 George Washington's Birthday

George Washington was born on February 11, 1731, but most reference books will tell you that he was born on February 22, 1732. Reference books may also tell you that Washington had no birthday in 1751. How can these facts be true?

The Julian calendar, which had been in use since the time of Julius Caesar, included a leap year every four years. However, this calendar had too many leap years, so it was out of <u>synchrony</u> with the solar year. In 1582 Pope Gregory XIII eliminated 10 days so the calendar would align with the seasons. To avoid gaining extra days in the future, he decreed that a century year would be a leap year only if the year was divisible by 400 (for example, the year 2000). In addition, he decided that New Year's Day would be January 1, not March 25 as it had been. But not all countries changed to the Gregorian calendar. When Washington was born, England—as well as its colonies—was still using the Julian calendar.

England decided to begin using the Gregorian calendar in 1752. By then the Julian calendar was 11 days behind the new calendar. Two adjustments had to be made to the 1752 calendar. First, the year 1752 had to begin on January 1. The year 1751, which began on March 25, would end on December 31. This meant that 1751 was only about nine months long and that Washington did not have a birthday that year. His 19th birthday was on February 11, 1750; his 20th birthday—365 days later—was on February 11, 1752. Second, 11 days had to be eliminated. It was decided that the day after September 2, 1752, would be September 14, 1752.

Historians have changed old dates so they agree with the Gregorian calendar. Washington's birthday was February 11, 1731, on the Julian calendar; it became February 22, 1732, on the Gregorian calendar.

Main Idea	1	Answer	Score
	Mark the *main idea*	M	15
	Mark the statement that is *too broad*	B	5
	Mark the statement that is *too narrow*	N	5

a. George Washington was born on February 11, 1731. ☐ ____

b. People have used various calendars over the centuries. ☐ ____

c. Washington's birth date changed because of the Gregorian calendar. ☐ ____

Subject Matter   **2**   Another good title for this passage might be
- [ ] a. Switching to the Gregorian Calendar.
- [ ] b. Switching to the Julian Calendar.
- [ ] c. Pope Gregory XIII.
- [ ] d. The American Colonies.

_____

Supporting Details   **3**   Washington changed his birth year from
- [ ] a. 1582 to 1731.
- [ ] b. 1731 to 1732.
- [ ] c. 1732 to 1731.
- [ ] d. 1600 to 2000.

_____

Conclusion   **4**   It is likely that the English colonies switched to the Gregorian calendar in 1752 because
- [ ] a. England switched then.
- [ ] b. the Romans switched then.
- [ ] c. they were at war with England.
- [ ] d. George Washington recommended it.

_____

Clarifying Devices   **5**   The writer uses the story of George Washington
- [ ] a. to give a specific example of how the Gregorian calendar caused changes.
- [ ] b. because he was our first president.
- [ ] c. because no one is sure what year he died.
- [ ] d. to explain why the Julian calendar was used for so long.

_____

Vocabulary in Context   **6**   <u>Synchrony</u> is the state of
- [ ] a. occurring in an oval pattern.
- [ ] b. occurring together.
- [ ] c. being completely separate.
- [ ] d. being enemies.

_____

Add your scores for questions 1–6. Enter the total here and on the graph on page 159.   **Total Score**   _____

45 Who Drinks Mineral Water?

The following puzzle is a variation of a brain-strainer entitled "Who Owns the Zebra?" It begins with this premise: *In San Francisco, three Victorian mansions stand in a row, each painted a different color and inhabited by a homeowner of a different nationality. Each householder owns a different exotic pet and drinks a different beverage.*

Here are the clues and the puzzle to be solved. (1) The Brazilian resides in the vermilion mansion. (2) The Vietnamese coddles the kangaroo. (3) Cappuccino is elegantly sipped in the magenta mansion. (4) The Vietnamese drinks pomegranate nectar. (5) The chartreuse mansion stands immediately to the right of the vermilion one. (6) The Dalmatian owner <u>imbibes</u> cappuccino. (7) The chimpanzee owner resides in the splendid vermilion edifice. (8) Pomegranate nectar is drunk in the mansion on the far right. Now: *Who drinks mineral water, and in which house does the Ukrainian live?*

Two essentials for working out a puzzle such as this include charting information into categories and discarding clues that are irrelevant. A careful reading of the puzzle's original premise reveals the categories below.

nationality   house   color   pet   drink

Once these categories are established, it is a fairly simple matter to chart the information provided by the clues and discover unfilled spots in the puzzle, which would reveal the answers. But you also need to recognize the unnecessary clues about the position of the houses. By identifying those clues, numbers 5 and 8, and then discarding them, you should be able to quickly come up with a solution.

Main Idea   1

	Answer	Score
Mark the *main idea*	M	15
Mark the statement that is *too broad*	B	5
Mark the statement that is *too narrow*	N	5

a. Solving logic puzzles requires categorizing information and eliminating irrelevant details. ☐ _____

b. The Brazilian lives in the vermilion mansion. ☐ _____

c. Logic puzzles can be entertaining to solve. ☐ _____

Score 15 points for each correct answer.   **Score**

Subject Matter **2** Another good title for this passage might be
- [ ] a. Owning an Exotic Pet.
- [ ] b. Solving a Logic Puzzle.
- [ ] c. A List of Facts and Details.
- [ ] d. Splendid Victorian Mansions.

_____

Supporting Details **3** The Vietnamese homeowner
- [ ] a. lives in an elegant magenta mansion.
- [ ] b. owns a chimpanzee.
- [ ] c. drinks pomegranate nectar.
- [ ] d. does not live near the Ukrainian.

_____

Conclusion **4** The blanks in a completed diagram would reveal
- [ ] a. where *Ukrainian* and *mineral water* belong.
- [ ] b. that the puzzle cannot be solved.
- [ ] c. the positions of the various houses.
- [ ] d. how many chimpanzees there were.

_____

Clarifying Devices **5** The last sentence of the passage is intended to
- [ ] a. challenge you to solve the puzzle yourself.
- [ ] b. confuse you.
- [ ] c. tell you what the solution is.
- [ ] d. prove that the puzzle is difficult.

_____

Vocabulary in Context **6** Imbibes means
- [ ] a. buys.
- [ ] b. sells.
- [ ] c. drinks.
- [ ] d. hates.

_____

Add your scores for questions 1–6. Enter the total here and on the graph on page 159. **Total Score** _____

46 Getting out of Credit Card Debt

Geraldine Ghirardelli was $2,500 in debt to a company called BicentennialCard when she received an introductory offer from MillenniumCard Corporation of a six-month 3.9 percent payment rate on balance transfers. In February Gerri transferred her balance to MillenniumCard, and MillenniumCard paid BicentennialCard $2,500 on March 1. Gerri's intent was to pay off her debt during the six-month period of MillenniumCard's special rate. Fortunately, she had just obtained a <u>lucrative</u> position in a telecommunications firm that enabled her to make substantial monthly payments.

Gerri correctly estimated that as long as she didn't make any additional charges on the card, six payments of $425, or a total payment of $2,550, would get her out of debt in time. Gerri arrived at her estimate this way. She multiplied the amount of the debt times the percentage rate for the loan ($2,500 × .039), for a total of $97.50, then divided that amount by 2 (because she was only paying for half of the year). Rounding her total of $48.75 up to $50, Gerri paid that amount in interest over the six months and was able to retire her debt.

It was worth it for Gerri to stretch a little to pay off what she owed, and getting that low interest rate was a particularly lucky break. A more typical rate is about 17.5 percent. If Gerri had tried to pay off her debt in six months at that level, she would have estimated her total interest payments to be $218.75. This estimate gives you a good idea of how quickly interest on a debt piles up. And remember, the estimate of $218.75 would hold only if you didn't make any more purchases on the card. With every new purchase, the credit card company, through complicated formulas, adds interest to your debt. It is a good idea to follow Gerri's lead and pay off those credit cards.

Main Idea	1		
		Answer	**Score**
	Mark the *main idea*	M	15
	Mark the statement that is *too broad*	B	5
	Mark the statement that is *too narrow*	N	5
	a. Gerri owed $2,500 to a credit card company.	☐	___
	b. It is wise to get out of credit card debt as Gerri did.	☐	___
	c. Many people owe on credit cards.	☐	___

Score 15 points for each correct answer.   Score

Subject Matter 2 Another good title for this passage might be
☐ a. Looking Closely at Credit Card Bills.
☐ b. Working in Telecommunications.
☐ c. The BicentennialCard Company.
☐ d. The MillenniumCard Corporation.   _____

Supporting Details 3 The $50 interest charge that Gerri estimated was
☐ a. at a 17.5 percent interest rate.
☐ b. at a 3.9 percent interest rate.
☐ c. for a loan she would pay off in one year.
☐ d. for a $2,550 debt.   _____

Conclusion 4 If $218.75 was the interest on a loan for six months, the interest for one year would be
☐ a. the same.
☐ b. half that much.
☐ c. three times that much.
☐ d. twice that much.   _____

Clarifying Devices 5 BicentennialCard and MillenniumCard are
☐ a. new credit card companies.
☐ b. credit card companies that have been forced out of business.
☐ c. names made up for the sake of the story.
☐ d. credit card companies with no membership charges.   _____

Vocabulary in Context 6 In this passage, <u>lucrative</u> means
☐ a. creative.
☐ b. secretarial.
☐ c. well-paying.
☐ d. stressful.   _____

Add your scores for questions 1–6. Enter the total here and on the graph on page 159.   Total Score   _____

47 Thinking in the Metric System

Although the units and relationships of the metric system have been taught in U.S. schools since the mid-1970s, most people in the United States have little or no "feeling" for metric units. They have no immediate answers for such questions as How many grams does a small dog weigh? or How many centimeters wide is a standard kitchen countertop? or Is 100 liters of water enough to fill a bathtub?

To develop a feeling for metric units, you can choose what are called *benchmarks*. These are known quantities that you memorize and then use to estimate other lengths, weights, and capacities. Common objects make good choices for benchmarks, since they are things that people are familiar with. For example, one centimeter measures about the width of a fingernail. A meter is about the height of a kitchen countertop, so that height can be your benchmark for to remembering the size of one meter. For a benchmark to be helpful, clearly it must be something that is familiar to *you*. For instance, if you like track and field events, you might pace off 100 meters, get a mental sense of how long this measurement is, and use it in estimating longer distances.

Centimeters and meters, as well as kilometers, measure length or distance. You'll also need benchmarks for capacity and weight, measured in metric units by liters or milliliters (capacity) and grams or kilograms (weight). Plastic soft drink bottles that hold two liters have become extremely common. <u>Couple</u> that knowledge with the fact that two liters equals 2,000 milliliters and you have one benchmark for liquid capacity; another benchmark might be the 200–300 milliliters of liquid in a water glass or coffee cup. And for estimating weights? A cordless phone handset is about 25 grams, and 100 pounds is about 45 kilograms—either of these facts can help you choose a weight benchmark.

Main Idea	1		
		Answer	**Score**
	Mark the *main idea*	M	15
	Mark the statement that is *too broad*	B	5
	Mark the statement that is *too narrow*	N	5

    a. Choosing personal benchmarks can help you understand the metric system. ☐ _____

    b. You need benchmarks for capacity and weight. ☐ _____

    c. Many systems of measurement exist. ☐

Subject Matter   **2**   This passage is mostly concerned with
- [ ] a. adding and subtracting in the metric system.
- [ ] b. ways of getting more familiar with the metric system.
- [ ] c. finding out how much certain objects weigh.
- [ ] d. why yards are easier than meters.   _____

Supporting Details   **3**   The height of a countertop is a good benchmark for a
- [ ] a. gram.
- [ ] b. centimeter.
- [ ] c. meter.
- [ ] d. kilometer.   _____

Conclusion   **4**   The author of this passages believes that
- [ ] a. the metric system is a waste of time.
- [ ] b. if you use benchmarks, you'll never have to measure.
- [ ] c. the metric system is are commonly used by people in the United States.
- [ ] d. people should have some knowledge of the metric system.   _____

Clarifying Devices   **5**   The examples in the first paragraph show that most people
- [ ] a. have never heard of the metric system.
- [ ] b. have trouble estimating with metric units.
- [ ] c. think length and distance are different things.
- [ ] d. think weight and capacity are the same thing.   _____

Vocabulary in Context   **6**   In this passage, the word <u>couple</u> means
- [ ] a. a man and woman who are dating.
- [ ] b. to link together or connect.
- [ ] c. a piece that holds two train cars together.
- [ ] d. a few.   _____

Add your scores for questions 1–6. Enter the total here and on the graph on page 159.   **Total Score**   _____

48 Winning Combinations

Francisca Rodrigues was a fast runner. She considered entering the 100-meter race in the local Teenage Olympics. She learned that 45 people had applied to compete in the race. Francisca wondered how many possible ways there were for this <u>substantial</u> group of runners to win first-, second-, and third-place medals.

Francisca's teacher explained that she could find the number of possible winning arrangements by multiplying. For example, suppose there were just three runners—A, B, and C—in a race. Any of the three would be a possible first-place winner. Once the first-place winner was determined, the two remaining runners would be possible second-place winners. That would leave just one possible third-place winner. So three runners could finish in one of the following ways:

A B C	B C A	C B A
A C B	B A C	C A B

The multiplication equation for this problem is $3 \times 2 \times 1 = 6$.

Since there were 45 entrants in the 100-meter race, there were 45 possibilities for first place. That left 44 second-place possibilities and 43 third-place possibilities. To find out the total number of ways 45 runners could finish first, second, and third, Francisca did the following multiplication: $45 \times 44 \times 43$. To her surprise, there were 85,140 possible combinations of first-, second-, and third-place winners.

After qualifying rounds were held, only 10 runners were actually entered in the 100-meter race. Francisca was one of them. To find out the number of possibilities for first-, second-, and third-place combinations of 10 runners, she multiplied $10 \times 9 \times 8$. There were 720 possibilities.

Main Idea 1

	Answer	Score
Mark the *main idea*	M	15
Mark the statement that is *too broad*	B	5
Mark the statement that is *too narrow*	N	5

a. The number of possible arrangements of first-, second-, and third-place winners in a race depends on the number of runners. ☐ ____

b. Francisca was interested in running. ☐ ____

c. With 45 runners, there were 85,140 possible combinations of winners. ☐ ____

Score 15 points for each correct answer.   Score

Subject Matter   **2**   Another good title for this passage might be
- ☐ a. The 10 Runners.
- ☐ b. The Teenage Olympics.
- ☐ c. Winning Possibilities.
- ☐ d. Winning a Medal.   _____

Supporting Details   **3**   With 10 runners competing in the 100-meter-race,
- ☐ a. there would be more than 85,000 possible arrangements of first-, second-, and third-place winners.
- ☐ b. the field was very crowded.
- ☐ c. there would be 720 possible arrangements of first-, second-, and third-place winners.
- ☐ d. more than three runners are guaranteed to win medals.   _____

Conclusion   **4**   You could determine the number of ways that a group of 20 runners could place first, second, or third in a race by
- ☐ a. adding 20 + 19 + 18.
- ☐ b. dividing the number of runners by the number of places.
- ☐ c. multiplying 20×3.
- ☐ d. multiplying $20 \times 19 \times 18$.   _____

Clarifying Devices   **5**   The term _qualifying rounds_ means
- ☐ a. preliminary races run to eliminate contestants.
- ☐ b. the length of time before a race.
- ☐ c. races run in a circle.
- ☐ d. the length and shape of the course.   _____

Vocabulary   **6**   Substantial means
- ☐ a. superior.
- ☐ b. athletic.
- ☐ c. very large.
- ☐ d. differing from one to another.   _____

Add your scores for questions 1–6. Enter the total here and on the graph on page 159.   Total Score   _____

49 What a Coincidence!

Janella Molina, a veterinarian, was on a flight from Minneapolis to Albuquerque. Her seatmate was Stephanie Watanabe, a kindergarten teacher from Honolulu who now worked in San Diego. The two women were strangers; however, they were about the same age and both were nervous flyers, so they struck up a conversation. When the pilot pointed out a mountain range below, they began talking about Yosemite National Park. Janella's cousin and her husband, Carmina and Santiago, had recently gone camping there with another couple, Santiago's brother and his wife. Stephanie remarked that a first-grade teacher from her school had also recently visited Yosemite and had told Stephanie about a park ranger she had met there named Danielle Boone. Janella was <u>flabbergasted</u> when she heard this, but not just because the ranger's name was humorous. "That's amazing—I think my cousin ran into the same ranger!" she exclaimed. Soon Janella and Stephanie figured out something even more incredible: Stephanie's coworker was none other than Carmina's sister-in-law (she was married to Janella's cousin's husband's brother)!

It's likely that this story reminds you of a similar occurrence in your own life. In fact, everyone you know probably has a comparable anecdote to relate. This is because of the simple mathematics behind such coincidences, which really aren't so remarkable after all. Let's say you know about 1,500 people who are somewhat spread out around the United States. You meet a stranger and discover that one of the people you know knows one of the people he or she knows. If the stranger, like you, knows about 1,500 people, then there are 1,500 $\times$ 1,500 (or 2,250,000) opportunities for connections between your friends, family members, and acquaintances and those of the stranger. It is likely that at least one connection will exist.

Main Idea	1			
			Answer	**Score**
	Mark the *main idea*		M	15
	Mark the statement that is *too broad*		B	5
	Mark the statement that is *too narrow*		N	5

    a. Janella's cousin and Stephanie's co-worker were at Yosemite together. ☐ _____

    b. It is likely that two strangers will find people they know in common. ☐ _____

    c. Coincidences occur quite often. ☐ _____

Subject Matter 2 This passage is primarily about
- [ ] a. making friends on airline flights.
- [ ] b. multiplying large numbers.
- [ ] c. the likelihood of connections between strangers.
- [ ] d. how amazing it is that Janella had a connection to Stephanie.

_____

Supporting Details 3 Janella and Stephanie were connected because
- [ ] a. one's cousin had married the other's brother.
- [ ] b. they both knew Danielle Boone.
- [ ] c. they had each visited Yosemite.
- [ ] d. they knew people who visited Yosemite at the same time.

_____

Conclusion 4 The writer wants us to conclude that
- [ ] a. coincidences are not as amazing as we think.
- [ ] b. coincidences are even more remarkable than we think.
- [ ] c. Janella and Stephanie had met before.
- [ ] d. Danielle Boone was from Kentucky.

_____

Clarifying Devices 5 The first paragraph is developed mainly through
- [ ] a. comparing and contrasting.
- [ ] b. listing the steps in a process.
- [ ] c. relating an anecdote.
- [ ] d. providing details to support a main idea.

_____

Vocabulary in Context 6 The word <u>flabbergasted</u> means
- [ ] a. obese.
- [ ] b. surprised.
- [ ] c. amused.
- [ ] d. frightened.

_____

Add your scores for questions 1–6. Enter the total here and on the graph on page 159.   **Total Score**

_____

50 Avoiding Supermarket Booby Traps

On your next visit to your local supermarket, be aware that it has probably been booby trapped (by marketing experts) with ingenious features designed to lengthen your stay and entice you to spend your money freely.

What sights and smells greet you upon entering a supermarket? Chances are it's those of the bakery or floral section. Exquisitely displayed bouquets or freshly baked cinnamon rolls can send <u>subliminal</u> messages to customers: "This is a classy store! Go ahead and pamper yourself—you deserve a treat! Who cares about the cost?"

If parents are softhearted and their kids are drawn to bright packages decorated with zany cartoon characters, it's probably best to leave the kids at home. Many stores place "kid friendly" products such as sugary breakfast cereals where kids are most likely to see them—and begin clamoring for them. Don't be surprised if you have to stretch to reach the Health Farm High-Fiber Crunchies, while the Sugar-Sparkled Choco Krispies are right there at children's eye level.

Supermarkets profit when patrons linger longer. That's why you'll often see cartons of merchandise stacked artistically in the aisles, partially blocking your way and creating a warehouse atmosphere that whispers "This store is chock-full of bargains!" Impulse buys such as pricey gourmet salad dressing or expensive imported marmalade are usually prominently placed at the very beginning of an aisle or on an endcap, a special display area at the head or foot of an aisle.

If you're interested in saving money, practice dodging these marketing booby traps. One possible antidote to impulse buying is to eat heartily *before* you go grocery shopping. Just think how smug you'll feel when you outsmart the marketing experts!

Main Idea	1	Answer	Score
	Mark the *main idea*	M	15
	Mark the statement that is *too broad*	B	5
	Mark the statement that is *too narrow*	N	5
	a. Marketing makes people buy.	☐	____
	b. "Kid friendly" products are placed at kids' eye level.	☐	____
	c. Be aware of marketing methods used in supermarkets.	☐	____

Subject Matter 2 This passage is mainly about
- ☐ a. marketing experts.
- ☐ b. flowers sold in supermarkets.
- ☐ c. supermarket architecture.
- ☐ d. supermarket marketing techniques. _____

Supporting Details 3 An endcap is a display area located
- ☐ a. in front of a supermarket.
- ☐ b. in the middle of an aisle, at eye level.
- ☐ c. at children's eye level.
- ☐ d. at the head or foot of an aisle. _____

Conclusion 4 The writer probably wants to help readers
- ☐ a. locate supermarkets that do not use marketing techniques.
- ☐ b. know the challenges of store design.
- ☐ c. avoid buying items they don't really need.
- ☐ d. learn how to become supermarket managers. _____

Clarifying Devices 5 The writer uses the idea of booby traps to
- ☐ a. remind shoppers to avoid slipping on slick floors.
- ☐ b. represent marketing techniques.
- ☐ c. represent methods of saving money.
- ☐ d. suggest that supermarkets have poor safety records. _____

Vocabulary in Context 6 In this passage, <u>subliminal</u> means
- ☐ a. fragrant.
- ☐ b. unconscious.
- ☐ c. bright.
- ☐ d. garbled. _____

Add your scores for questions 1–6. Enter the total here and on the graph on page 159.   **Total Score** _____

51 Get Me to the Airport on Time

People overestimate and underestimate constantly. Whether you over- or under-estimate depends on whether you prefer to end up with a surplus or a <u>dearth</u>.

Liz Wolski is a restaurateur whose well-run cafe features a daily fish special. Liz feels that it is essential for fish to be extremely fresh. Unfortunately, she says, even well-refrigerated fresh fish often tastes "fishy" on the second day. Thus Liz habitually underestimates the number of customers who will order the fish special each day. She would rather disappoint some patrons than waste food and money. Also, she's confident that most customers will be willing to order something else.

Al Conway is a business executive whose position requires frequent travel. Al absolutely detests waiting at the airport for flights to leave. As a result, he always used to depart for the airport at the last possible moment. By cutting his time so close, he occasionally missed flights altogether. Conway's wife Mary (who often drives him to the airport) finally put her foot down and refused to take him under such stressful conditions. As a result, Al reluctantly pledged that in the future he would leave for the airport with plenty of time to spare.

Overestimating or underestimating can lead to wasted food or money, missed airline flights, or even disaster. (According to some, the designers of the *Titanic* purposefully underestimated the number of lifeboats needed to accommodate all passengers.) However, carefully considered over- or underestimating can help people function more effectively. The next time you're uncertain whether to overestimate or underestimate, use the following formula: *If I end up with too much _____, then A will happen; if I end up with too little of it, then B will happen. I would rather have A happen than B (or vice versa).*

Main Idea   1

	Answer	Score
Mark the *main idea*	M	15
Mark the statement that is *too broad*	B	5
Mark the statement that is *too narrow*	N	5

a. Liz saves money by underestimating.	☐	____
b. Judicious estimating helps people function well.	☐	____
c. Most people estimate frequently.	☐	____

Subject Matter   **2**   Another good title for this passage might be
- [ ] a. Don't Overestimate!
- [ ] b. Enough, Too Little, or Too Much?
- [ ] c. Liz's Restaurant.
- [ ] d. Fresh out of Fresh Fish.

_____

Supporting Details   **3**   Al underestimated the amount of time it would take to get to the airport because
- [ ] a. he was not good at keeping track of time.
- [ ] b. his wife always drove too slowly.
- [ ] c. he hated to wait for flights to leave.
- [ ] d. it took him a long time to pack.

_____

Conclusion   **4**   We can conclude from the passage that it would be wise to overestimate when calculating the amount of
- [ ] a. time needed to complete a project with a strict deadline.
- [ ] b. cash to withdraw from a local ATM.
- [ ] c. perishable food to buy for a beach picnic.
- [ ] d. time children will spend on chores.

_____

Clarifying Devices   **5**   The second and third paragraphs are included to
- [ ] a. provide contrast to the first paragraph.
- [ ] b. relate a humorous anecdote.
- [ ] c. explain the steps in a process.
- [ ] d. provide examples.

_____

Vocabulary in Context   **6**   Dearth means
- [ ] a. fiasco.
- [ ] b. excess.
- [ ] c. lack.
- [ ] d. murder.

_____

Add your scores for questions 1–6. Enter the total here and on the graph on page 160.   **Total Score**

_____

52 Brother, Can You Spare $100,000?

Demetrius Dembowski has obtained a 30-year fixed-rate home loan of $100,000 with an annual interest rate of 7.5 percent. Because Demetrius owes more money at the begining of the 30 years than at the end, he pays more interest at first. Thus in the beginning months, Dembowski's principal payment—the amount he pays toward his actual loan—increases extremely slowly.

Payment Number	Total Monthly Payment	Principal Portion of Payment	Interest Portion of Payment	Current Balance
1	$699.21	$ 74.21	$625.00	$99,925.79
2	$699.21	$ 74.68	$624.54	$99,851.11
359	$699.21	$690.56	$ 8.66	$ 694.87
360	$699.21	$694.87	$ 4.34	$ 0.00

Let's analyze Demetrius's early payments. Imagine that on December 15 the Mauritanian Mortgage Corporation gives Demetrius $100,000 and on January 15 his initial payment is due. Throughout this first month, interest <u>accumulates</u> on the entire $100,000. On a yearly interest rate of 7.5%, Demetrius's monthly rate is 0.625%, or 7.5% divided by 12. Multiplying $100,000 by 0.625% yields $625, the portion of Demetrius's first monthly payment that is interest. So Demetrius now owes $100,625 ($100,000 + $625), and after his initial payment of $699.21, he still owes $99,925.79 ($100,625 − $699.21). His February interest payment will be .625% of $99,925.79.

By the time Dembowski makes his last few payments, his monthly interest payment has decreased considerably. His balance following his 359th payment is $694.87, and 0.625% of that is about $4.34, his final interest payment. What was the total amount of interest Demetrius paid? Multiplying 360 months by $699.21 equals $251,715.60, and subtracting $100,000 (the loan amount) leaves $151,715.60—more than 1.5 times what he actually borrowed!

Main Idea 1

	Answer	Score
Mark the *main idea*	M	15
Mark the statement that is *too broad*	B	5
Mark the statement that is *too narrow*	N	5

a. Demetrius took out a home loan. ☐ _____

b. The final interest payment was $4.34. ☐ _____

c. The interest on a large long-term loan decreases gradually over time. ☐ _____

Score 15 points for each correct answer.   **Score**

Subject Matter 2   This passage is mainly concerned with
- [ ] a. Demetrius Dembowski.
- [ ] b. the Mauritanian Mortgage Corporation.
- [ ] c. how interest payments on a loan change.
- [ ] d. calculating the number of payments Demetrius made.

_____

Supporting Details 3   The monthly interest rate on Demetrius's loan was
- [ ] a. 7.5%.
- [ ] b. 6.5%.
- [ ] c. 0.625%.
- [ ] d. $625.

_____

Conclusion 4   We can conclude that Demetrius's total monthly payment was always
- [ ] a. $699.21.
- [ ] b. $100,000.
- [ ] c. $360.
- [ ] d. $151,715.60.

_____

Clarifying Devices 5   The table in the passage helps the reader see
- [ ] a. Demetrius's down payment before he took out the loan.
- [ ] b. Demetrius's first and last interest payments.
- [ ] c. how much his interest payments increased.
- [ ] d. at what point the interest and principal payments were just about equal.

_____

Vocabulary in Context 6   Accumulates means
- [ ] a. fades away.
- [ ] b. builds up.
- [ ] c. gets used to.
- [ ] d. decreases.

_____

Add your scores for questions 1–6. Enter the total here and on the graph on page 160.   **Total Score**

_____

53 The Golden Rectangle

One of the most commonly used geometric shapes is the rectangle—a four-sided figure with four right angles. If you start looking for rectangular shapes in the physical world, you'll find them almost everywhere, perhaps because people are attracted to the precision and order conveyed by this shape. One way to classify a rectangle is by the ratio of its length to its width; for example, a square is a rectangle in which the ratio of the length to the width is 1 to 1. A rectangle with the length-width ratio 20 to 1 would be very long and skinny; one with the ratio 1.1 to 1 would be almost square.

Are some rectangular shapes more commonly used than others? In mathematics, one particular rectangle has been distinguished by being named "golden." In a golden rectangle, the length (L) and the width (W) must satisfy the proportion $W/L = L/(W + L)$. In other words, the ratio of the width to the length must be the same as the ratio of the length to the width-length sum. If W equals 1, then solving the formula for L results in approximately 1.618. Golden rectangles—rectangles with a length-width ratio of 1.618 to 1—have been found in art, architecture, and mathematical writings for more than 4,000 years, with one especially <u>notable</u> example being the base of the Parthenon in Athens, Greece.

Do you have golden rectangles in your home or where you work? To find out, simply divide the length of any rectangle by its width; if the quotient equals about 1.6, then you have a golden rectangle. Performing this division on a 5-by-3 index card results in the quotient 1.666 and performing it on an 8-by-5 card gives the quotient 1.6, so both of these shapes are close to being golden rectangles. With a ruler and a calculator, you can check your computer monitor, television screen, and the other rectangular shapes in your home and probably find quite a few additional examples.

Main Idea 1		Answer	Score
Mark the *main idea*		M	15
Mark the statement that is *too broad*		B	5
Mark the statement that is *too narrow*		N	5
a. Many common objects are rectangular.		☐	___
b. A 5-by-3 index card is almost a golden rectangle.		☐	___
c. Golden rectangles have a particular length-width ratio.		☐	___

Score 15 points for each correct answer.   **Score**

Subject Matter   **2**   This passage is mainly about
☐ a. identifying shapes that contain right angles.
☐ b. describing the proportions of golden rectangles.
☐ c. learning the sizes of index cards.
☐ d. solving formulas about rectangles.   _____

Supporting   **3**   The ratio of the length to the width of a square
Details   shape is
☐ a. equal to that of a golden rectangle.
☐ b. 1 to 20.
☐ c. 20 to 1.
☐ d. 1 to 1.   _____

Conclusion   **4**   Golden rectangles are found frequently in art and
architecture because
☐ a. their proportions are pleasing to the eye.
☐ b. people think they bring wealth or good luck.
☐ c. they can substitute for squares.
☐ d. they can be drawn without right angles.   _____

Clarifying   **5**   To find out if a rectangle is "golden," the writer
Devices   suggests
☐ a. using the formula $W/L = L/(W + L)$.
☐ b. measuring a shape and then using division.
☐ c. comparing it to the shape of the Parthenon.
☐ d. comparing it to the shape of a square.   _____

Vocabulary   **6**   In this passage, the word <u>notable</u> means
in Context   ☐ a. recorded.
☐ b. well-proportioned.
☐ c. important or worthy of notice.
☐ d. beautiful.   _____

Add your scores for questions 1–6. Enter the total here   **Total**
and on the graph on page 160.   **Score**   _____

54 Double or Nothing

Begin with a sheet of newspaper and cut it in half to get two pieces; then stack up the pieces and cut in half again to get four pieces. Continue this process until you can't cut the stack of paper anymore. How many times do you think you'll be able to repeat the process of doubling the number of pieces of paper? The doubling pattern that results from an activity of this type may surprise you in how quickly the numbers increase. In this example—where the <u>initial</u> number is 1—the resulting pattern is 1, 2, 4, 8, 16, 32, 64, and so on, with each number equaling twice that of the preceding number and the total quantity doubling at each step.

Doubling patterns are also called exponential patterns, because they can be represented by mathematical expressions such as 2^x. (The x, an exponent, indicates how many times a number should be used as a multiplying factor.) For example, let x equal each number in the sequence 1, 2, 3, and so forth. Substituting each number in the expression 2^x (2^1, 2^2 . . .) results in the same doubling pattern that develops in the newspaper cutting experiment: 2, 4, 8, 16, etc. Doubling patterns are among the simplest of the exponential relationships, so they are often used to introduce the concept of exponents in math classes and textbooks. Exponential relationships have numerous practical uses; in particular, the growth of populations is predicted using equations of this type.

The simple doubling pattern is the basis for many folktales and math puzzles. One folktale has a clever hero asking for a single grain of wheat on the first square of a chess board and then continually doubling the number until the 64-square board is full. A clever negotiator might agree to do a job for one penny on day one and then double the money each day until the job is done. A little experimentation with a calculator will show that such an agreement would result in more than 10 million dollars for a 30-day job!

Main Idea   1

	Answer	Score
Mark the *main idea*	**M**	15
Mark the statement that is *too broad*	**B**	5
Mark the statement that is *too narrow*	**N**	5

a. Number patterns have many uses. ☐ _____

b. One doubling pattern is 1, 2, 4, 8, etc. ☐ _____

c. In a doubling pattern, each number is twice that of the previous one. ☐ _____

Subject Matter   **2**   This passage is mostly concerned with
- ☐ a. describing population growth.
- ☐ b. multiplying numbers.
- ☐ c. explaining and showing uses for doubling patterns.
- ☐ d. showing how many folktales use math.   _____

Supporting Details   **3**   The mathematical expression 2^x represents
- ☐ a. a doubling pattern.
- ☐ b. a halving pattern.
- ☐ c. cutting a newspaper in pieces.
- ☐ d. $2 \times 2 \times 2 \times 2 \times 2$.   _____

Conclusion   **4**   In the doubling pattern 3, 6, 12, 24, etc., the next number would be
- ☐ a. 28.
- ☐ b. 36.
- ☐ c. 48.
- ☐ d. 64.   _____

Clarifying Devices   **5**   The first paragraph describes cutting a newspaper sheet in pieces in order to
- ☐ a. show how useful doubling patterns can be.
- ☐ b. show how to follow simple directions.
- ☐ c. make the reader laugh.
- ☐ d. demonstrate how a doubling pattern actually works.   _____

Vocabulary in Context   **6**   In this passage, <u>initial</u> means
- ☐ a. a letter representing a person's name.
- ☐ b. from the beginning of time.
- ☐ c. short and to the point.
- ☐ d. first.   _____

Add your scores for questions 1–6. Enter the total here and on the graph on page 160.   Total Score   _____

55 Can We Get Rid of Some Zeros?

What's the largest number you can think of? For most people, a number in the trillions is about the largest quantity they will ever encounter. One trillion is 1 followed by 12 zeroes, or, written out in numerals, a trillion is 1,000,000,000,000. Because numbers this large are awkward to write out, they are usually abbreviated in some manner. Often a decimal and a word form are used: 3.2 trillion means 3.2 times one trillion, or 3,200,000,000,000.

You might assume that <u>everyday</u> people could never do calculations with numbers this large; after all, an ordinary calculator displays only eight digits. You could not even enter 3.2 trillion into an ordinary calculator. Even using a calculator with a 12-digit display, a person doing calculations in the trillions would quickly run out of display space. It would seem that people working with numbers this large would need expensive computers for their work.

However, there are methods for doing computations with huge numbers that employ pocket-sized calculators and even paper-and-pencil techniques. The key to manipulating numbers of this sort involves writing them in a form called scientific notation. Scientific notation eliminates the need for writing out all the numerals in very large numbers and, what is even more useful, provides a way to do computations with these quantities. In scientific notation, 3.2 trillion is written as 3.2×10^{12}, with the exponent 12 representing the 12 zeros in one trillion. Multiplying numbers in scientific notation requires adding exponents. If 3.5 million people each got a tax refund of $2,000, the total refund would be 3.5×10^6 times 2.0×10^3, which equals 7×10^9. For anyone who works with really enormous quantities frequently, the effort required to learn scientific notation is more than offset by the ease and accuracy this form of numeral writing can provide.

Main Idea 1

	Answer	Score
Mark the *main idea*	M	15
Mark the statement that is *too broad*	B	5
Mark the statement that is *too narrow*	N	5

a. A trillion is 1 followed by 12 zeroes. ☐ ____

b. Exponents have many uses in math. ☐ ____

c. Scientific notation is a short way of writing very large numbers. ☐ ____

Score 15 points for each correct answer.   **Score**

Subject Matter 2 This passage is mostly concerned with
- ☐ a. explaining what exponents are.
- ☐ b. the names for very large numbers.
- ☐ c. why scientific notation is needed.
- ☐ d. being accurate when using calculators.   _____

Supporting Details 3 Multiplying of very large numbers is usually done
- ☐ a. on an eight-digit calculator.
- ☐ b. on an twelve-digit calculator.
- ☐ c. on a very large computer.
- ☐ d. with scientific notation.   _____

Conclusion 4 Which of these professions would most likely involve using scientific notation for numbers?
- ☐ a. treasurer of a local block club
- ☐ b. law enforcement
- ☐ c. building construction
- ☐ d. astronomy   _____

Clarifying Devices 5 The writer shows that numbers in scientific notation can be multiplied by
- ☐ a. demonstrating how to multiply two large numbers.
- ☐ b. explaining the steps on a calculator.
- ☐ c. writing long numbers in shorter forms.
- ☐ d. explaining how many zeroes are in a trillion.   _____

Vocabulary in Context 6 In this passage, everyday means
- ☐ a. done frequently.
- ☐ b. ordinary.
- ☐ c. poorly educated.
- ☐ d. routine.   _____

Add your scores for questions 1–6. Enter the total here and on the graph on page 160.   **Total Score**   _____

56 Birthday Twins

When was the last time you met someone who has the same birthday as you do, someone born on the same day who might be called your "birthday twin"? Since there are 365 different days in every year except leap year, common sense would suggest that encountering a birthday twin is a pretty rare occurrence. You might guess that you'd need to meet 365 people to be certain of finding just one person born on the same day that you were. In this situation, common sense would lead you <u>astray</u>. You do not need a group of 365 people to be reasonably certain of finding a pair of birthday twins—in fact, the size of the group needed is considerably smaller.

Finding the chances of two people in a group sharing the same birthday is a well-known problem in the area of mathematics called *probability*. To compute probabilities of this type, mathematicians make use of the concept of *complementary probabilities*. This states that the probability of an event happening plus the probability of the event not happening must equal 1. Think of 5 balls in a vase. If there are only 2 white balls, the probability of drawing a white ball is 2 chances out of 5, or the fraction $\frac{2}{5}$. The probability of *not* drawing a white ball is 3 chances out of 5, or $\frac{3}{5}$, and $\frac{2}{5}$ plus $\frac{3}{5}$ equals 1. For some complicated types of probability problems, it is easier to first find the chance of something *not* happening and then subtract that quantity from 1.

Using computational techniques that apply complementary probabilities, you would discover that the chances of two people in a group of just 30 persons sharing the same birthday is over 70 percent. To have an even chance, a chance of 50 percent, of finding birthday twins, all you actually need is a group of 24 people. The next time you attend a meeting or a party with more than 24 people, you might test this mathematical fact. Chances are good that two people in the group will be birthday twins.

Main Idea	1		
		Answer	**Score**
Mark the *main idea*		M	15
Mark the statement that is *too broad*		B	5
Mark the statement that is *too narrow*		N	5

a. The probability of two people sharing a birthday is higher than you might think. ☐ _____

b. People may share the same birthday. ☐ _____

c. Complementary probabilities add up to 1. ☐ _____

Subject Matter   2   This passage is mainly about

☐ a. how common sense helps with probabilities.

☐ b. adding up numbers to get 1.

☐ c. drawing or not drawing balls of a given color.

☐ d. the chances of two people in a group having the same birthday.   _____

Supporting Details   3   The probabilities $\frac{2}{5}$ and $\frac{3}{5}$ are complementary because

☐ a. they show that something is very likely to happen.

☐ b. when you subtract them, you get $\frac{1}{5}$.

☐ c. they add up to 1.

☐ d. they are both numbers less than 1.   _____

Conclusion   4   In a group of 100 people, the chances of two people sharing the same birthday are

☐ a. very low.

☐ b. about even.

☐ c. very high.

☐ d. certain.   _____

Clarifying Devices   5   The example of the white balls in the vase is used to

☐ a. show how to subtract fractions.

☐ b. explain complementary probabilities.

☐ c. demonstrate the uses of percentages.

☐ d. help solve the birthday problem.   _____

Vocabulary in Context   6   In this passage, <u>astray</u> means

☐ a. into error.

☐ b. into a dangerous situation.

☐ c. far away.

☐ d. toward a goal.   _____

Add your scores for questions 1–6. Enter the total here and on the graph on page 160.   **Total Score**   _____

57 Geometry on the Floor

When you move or rearrange the furniture in a room, two yardsticks and a pad of quarter-inch graph paper can prevent a tremendous amount of sweat and frustration, perhaps even an injured back! The yardsticks and graph paper are simple and inexpensive tools you can utilize to create a floor plan similar to the simplified sample shown in the illustration below.

When using the yardsticks to measure dimensions of rooms, lay the two measuring instruments end-to-end to measure six feet; move the first yardstick to get nine feet; and so forth. You'll discover that the two-stick method is more convenient than struggling with a very long tape measure, and it is a method easily <u>implemented</u> alone, whereas using a tape measure generally requires an additional person.

Use one square on the graph paper to stand for one square foot; then measure all distances and dimensions of furniture to the nearest half foot—that's close

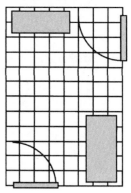

enough for most purposes and will make it easier to represent them on the floor plan. One mistake frequently made in planning room arrangements is to forget that a door takes up wall space when it is open. To avoid this mistake, use quarter-circle marks like the two shown in the sample floor plan to indicate the path of an opening door. If you look at the wall shown at the top of this sample, you'll notice that three feet of this wall are used when the door is open, thus leaving only five usable feet of space along this wall.

Main Idea	1	Answer	Score
	Mark the *main idea*	M	15
	Mark the statement that is *too broad*	B	5
	Mark the statement that is *too narrow*	N	5

a. Rooms can be drawn to proportion. ☐ ____

b. Drawing floor plans is simple to do and provides useful information. ☐ ____

c. Quarter-circles mark the openings of doors on floor plans. ☐ ____

Score 15 points for each correct answer.   **Score**

Subject Matter   **2**   This passage is mostly concerned with
☐ a. preventing back injuries when rearranging furniture.
☐ b. tips for making floor plans for rooms.
☐ c. geometric figures used in interior decorating.
☐ d. explaining uses of graph paper.   _____

Supporting Details   **3**   The floor plan included with this passage
☐ a. shows a room with only one door.
☐ b. includes all window openings.
☐ c. is for a room measuring 12 feet by 12 feet.
☐ d. uses one square to stand for one square foot.   _____

Conclusion   **4**   The two gray rectangles in the sample floor plan most likely show
☐ a. bookcases or cabinets.
☐ b. chairs or end tables.
☐ c. rugs.
☐ d. measuring sticks.   _____

Clarifying Devices   **5**   The writer explains how to use two yardsticks to measure a room dimension by
☐ a. recommending the use of a tape measure.
☐ b. giving an example.
☐ c. describing the procedure to use.
☐ d. showing a diagram.   _____

Vocabulary in Context   **6**   In this passage, the word <u>implemented</u> means
☐ a. understood.
☐ b. carried out.
☐ c. supplied with measuring tools.
☐ d. practiced.   _____

Add your scores for questions 1–6. Enter the total here and on the graph on page 160.   **Total Score**   _____

58 Good for Nothing?

Are there any practical purposes for the number zero, or could we function just as well without it? Zero describes the absence of something. While zero has a defined meaning on scales such as those used for temperature, in general it doesn't seem to be as useful as many other numbers.

If you concur with the notion that the number zero is not particularly valuable, you probably have not considered the most important use for this number, a use that you see every day and most likely take for granted. The number, or more precisely, the digit zero makes our positional system of numbers possible. Without zero, the numerals for three hundred two and for thirty-two would be indistinguishable from each other—and from many other numbers as well. The use of zero keeps the digits in their correct places so that the place value of each digit is immediately <u>apparent</u>. You know at a glance that the 3 in 302 has a value of 3 hundreds and not 3 thousands or 3 tenths or some other value. The place of each digit shows its value, and zeros keep the digits in the correct places.

So, what is so remarkable? you may be thinking. *Aren't all number systems positional with some kind of place-value system?* The truth is that not all number systems are place-value systems and that most very early number systems were not positional. Roman numerals, which are still used today for a few applications, are positional but do not include a symbol for zero. Egyptian numerals included no zero and had no positional values. One early number system that did include zero was that employed by the Maya in Central America. For the most part, however, the use of a symbol for zero was a relatively late introduction in methods used to record quantities.

Main Idea	1		
		Answer	**Score**
	Mark the *main idea*	M	15
	Mark the statement that is *too broad*	B	5
	Mark the statement that is *too narrow*	N	5
	a. All number systems vary somewhat.	☐	_____
	b. The zero in 302 separates the digits in the hundreds and ones places.	☐	_____
	c. Zero is needed to make our number-writing system work.	☐	_____

Subject Matter   **2**   Another good title for this passage would be
- [ ] a. What Is Place Value?
- [ ] b. Using Digits to Write Numbers.
- [ ] c. Number Systems Throughout History.
- [ ] d. The Importance of Zero.   ____

Supporting Details   **3**   The digit 3 in the number 302 has a value of three
- [ ] a. ones.
- [ ] b. tens.
- [ ] c. hundreds.
- [ ] d. hundredths.   ____

Conclusion   **4**   In a positional number system, the value of a symbol
- [ ] a. is always greater than zero.
- [ ] b. is sometimes equal to zero.
- [ ] c. indicates a large number.
- [ ] d. changes depending on its position.   ____

Clarifying Devices   **5**   The writer shows that zero is needed
- [ ] a. in every type of number system.
- [ ] b. to compare numbers.
- [ ] c. to make a number system positional.
- [ ] d. because the Maya used it.   ____

Vocabulary in Context   **6**   In this passage, <u>apparent</u> means
- [ ] a. wearable.
- [ ] b. complicated.
- [ ] c. understood.
- [ ] d. written in numbers.   ____

Add your scores for questions 1–6. Enter the total here and on the graph on page 160.   **Total Score**   ____

59 Two Types of Spirals

The grooves on an old-fashioned phonograph record and the shape of our galaxy—what can these two things possibly have in common? The title of this passage suggests the answer—that both a record and the Milky Way are examples of spirals. Spirals are also found in the shapes of shells, in the growth patterns of plants and trees, and in some spider webs.

You might think that the mathematics needed to describe these fascinating shapes is complicated, with many difficult formulas, but that is not the case. The two principal types of spirals, one tight and the other loose and loopy, can be simply explained using arithmetic and geometric number sequences.

In an arithmetic sequence, numbers are separated by a common difference—in the sequence 3, 6, 9, 12, that difference is 3. In a geometric sequence, such as 1, 2, 4, 8, the numbers are all multiplied by the same number, in this case 2. To draw a tight spiral as in a phonograph record, make a larger version of the polar coordinate grid at the right and plot a point every 10 degrees. The first point would be at the center, the second 3 units (or circles) away from it, the third 6 units away, and so on. For a galaxy spiral, again plot a point every 10 degrees but use a geometric sequence, placing the points 1, 2, 4, 8, etc., units from the center.

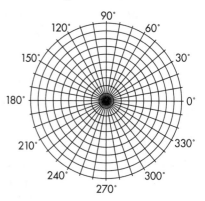

Main Idea 1

	Answer	Score
Mark the *main idea*	M	15
Mark the statement that is *too broad*	B	5
Mark the statement that is *too narrow*	N	5

a. Spirals can be found in nature and drawn using mathematics. ☐ _____

b. Mathematicians study many different complex curved shapes. ☐ _____

c. Spirals may be tight or loose and loopy. ☐ _____

Subject Matter   **2**   This passage is primarily concerned with
☐ a. explaining a polar coordinate grid.
☐ b. describing shapes of galaxies.
☐ c. describing how to create two types of spirals.
☐ d. measuring spirals in degrees.   _____

Supporting   **3**   The spiraling galaxy that includes our solar
Details   system is called
☐ a. Archimedean.
☐ b. geometric.
☐ c. polar.
☐ d. the Milky Way.   _____

Conclusion   **4**   Compared with a phonograph-record-shaped
spiral, a spiral in a galaxy shape would look
☐ a. looser.
☐ b. tighter.
☐ c. smaller.
☐ d. the same.   _____

Clarifying   **5**   The author includes the polar coordinate grid
Devices   ☐ a. to show a spiral drawn on it.
☐ b. so you would know how to draw it if you
wanted to create your own spirals.
☐ c. to show the shape of a phonograph record.
☐ d. to prove there are only two types of spirals.   _____

Vocabulary   **6**   In this passage, the word <u>plot</u> means
in Context   ☐ a. locate on a graph or grid.
☐ b. a piece of land.
☐ c. the events in a story.
☐ d. scheme.   _____

Add your scores for questions 1–6. Enter the total here   **Total**
and on the graph on page 160.   **Score**   _____

60 Just Like Jack and the Beanstalk

Giants figure prominently in children's stories, usually in an extremely negative role. You probably read such tales in your early years and enjoyed rooting for the "little guy" who plots to outwit the evil giant. Are such tremendously enlarged copies of human beings actually possible, or do they only exist in the imagination?

An examination of what happens to surface areas and volumes as you enlarge a three-dimensional geometric figure can help to permanently banish the idea of giants from our everyday world. Begin with a cube with a length, width, and height of 5 feet and then double those three dimensions—that is, multiply them by 2. The result when you do this is that the surface area increases by the square of 2 (2^2), or becomes four times as large. The volume increases by the cube of 2 (2^3), or becomes eight times as large. (You can prove to yourself that these conclusions are valid by computing the surface areas and volumes of the original cube as well as of the enlarged one. Use the formulas $A = S^2$ and $V = S^3$.)

So how does this information <u>translate</u> to giants? Think for a moment about the human body as it is scaled upward to giant-sized dimensions. The weight, or volume, of the body will increase eightfold, but the *strength* of the body will increase only with the cross-sectional surface area of the bones; that is, it will only increase fourfold. The weight will be so much greater than the strength that a giant couldn't stand or walk, much less threaten a person of standard dimensions.

The fact that giant-sized villains appear to be structurally impossible without some newly engineered increase in bone strength may occur to you the next time you hear a tale with a giant villain, but this scientific knowledge probably will not prevent you from enjoying the story anyway.

Main Idea	1		
		Answer	Score
Mark the *main idea*		M	15
Mark the statement that is *too broad*		B	5
Mark the statement that is *too narrow*		N	5

a. As the dimensions of a cube are doubled, volume increases eightfold. ☐ _____

b. Solid objects have length, surface area, and volume. ☐ _____

c. A simple enlarging experiment can explain why giants are not possible. ☐ _____

Subject Matter   2   Another good title for this passage would be
- [ ] a. Why Giants Are Always Evil.
- [ ] b. Finding the Volume of a Giant.
- [ ] c. Are Giants Possible?
- [ ] d. Famous Giants in Folktales.

_____

Supporting Details   3   If the dimensions of a cube were doubled, its surface area would become
- [ ] a. twice as large.
- [ ] b. four times as large.
- [ ] c. eight times as large.
- [ ] d. twelve times as large.

_____

Conclusion   4   A giant would not be strong enough to stand because
- [ ] a. its legs would be short.
- [ ] b. its bones could not support its weight.
- [ ] c. it would be too tall.
- [ ] d. its bones would be too thick.

_____

Clarifying Devices   5   The example used to make the point about giants is
- [ ] a. a square 2 feet on each side.
- [ ] b. a square 5 feet on each side.
- [ ] c. a cube 2 feet on each edge.
- [ ] d. a cube 5 feet on each edge.

_____

Vocabulary in Context   6   In this passage, <u>translate</u> means
- [ ] a. change from one language into another.
- [ ] b. carry from one place to another.
- [ ] c. relate to or correspond to.
- [ ] d. change from numbers into words.

_____

Add your scores for questions 1–6. Enter the total here and on the graph on page 160.   **Total Score**   _____

61 The Toss of a Coin

In a coin-tossing experiment involving one coin, the probability of the coin landing heads up is expressed by the fraction $\frac{1}{2}$. If there is more than one coin involved, is the probability of getting all heads still represented by this same fraction? To determine probability in more complex situations, it is necessary first to <u>ascertain</u> the possible ways in which the experimental coins can land. For an experiment consisting of two coins, there are just four distinguishable ways that the coins can land—HH, HT, TH, and TT. This information can be represented by the sequence 1, 2, 1 because there is 1 way of getting two heads-up coins (HH), 2 ways of getting one heads-up coin (HT or TH), and 1 way of getting zero heads-up coins (TT). This number sequence 1, 2, 1 can be used to determine the numerators in the four probability fractions, with the denominator of each fraction being the sum of the three numbers—1 + 2 + 1, or 4. The probability of getting two heads-up coins is therefore the fractional number $\frac{1}{4}$; of getting one heads-up coin, $\frac{2}{4}$ or $\frac{1}{2}$; and of getting none, $\frac{1}{4}$.

As the number of coins in the experiment increases, the probability fractions can be found by using a device called Pascal's Triangle, an arrangement of numbers in which each number is the sum of the two numbers directly above it. The fourth row of Pascal's Triangle is used for determining the probability fractions for a three-coin experiment. The denominator of the fractions is the sum of the numbers in the row; the numerators are the four numbers in the row. Following this procedure, you would discover that when tossing three coins, the probability of getting three heads is $\frac{1}{8}$; of getting two heads is $\frac{3}{8}$; of getting one head is $\frac{3}{8}$; and of getting no heads is $\frac{1}{8}$. The greater the number of coins, the lower the probability of getting all heads, as extending Pascal's Triangle for yourself would prove.

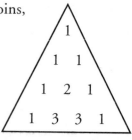

Main Idea

1 ——————————————————————

	Answer	Score
Mark the *main idea*	**M**	15
Mark the statement that is *too broad*	**B**	5
Mark the statement that is *too narrow*	**N**	5

a. Pascal's Triangle can be used to write probabilities in coin-toss experiments. ☐ ____

b. Probability shows up in coin tossing. ☐ ____

c. Two coins can fall HH, HT, TH, or TT. ☐ ____

Subject Matter   **2**   This passage is mostly concerned with
- [ ] a. definitions of terms used in probability.
- [ ] b. understanding numerators and denominators.
- [ ] c. finding probabilities in coin-tossing experiments.
- [ ] d. methods for constructing Pascal's Triangle.   _____

Supporting Details   **3**   You toss two coins. The probability that only one of the coins lands heads up is
- [ ] a. $\frac{1}{8}$.
- [ ] b. $\frac{1}{4}$.
- [ ] c. $\frac{1}{2}$.
- [ ] d. $\frac{3}{8}$.   _____

Conclusion   **4**   The next row of Pascal's Triangle will contain
- [ ] a. 5 numbers.
- [ ] b. 6 numbers.
- [ ] c. 2 numbers.
- [ ] d. 1 number.   _____

Clarifying Devices   **5**   The information in this passage is arranged from
- [ ] a. simplest to most difficult.
- [ ] b. most difficult to easiest.
- [ ] c. earliest to latest.
- [ ] d. latest to earliest.   _____

Vocabulary in Context   **6**   In this passage, the word <u>ascertain</u> means to
- [ ] a. deny.
- [ ] b. compute.
- [ ] c. find out.
- [ ] d. divide.   _____

Add your scores for questions 1–6. Enter the total here and on the graph on page 160.   **Total Score**   _____

62 Drawing on the Definition

If you are ever uncertain about how to draw a particular geometric shape, you can rely on the fact that definitions of geometric figures usually indicate how to draw or construct them. Familiar examples include the square ("four right angles and four equal sides"), the rectangle ("four right angles and opposite sides parallel"), and the right triangle ("one right angle and three sides of any length"). Curved figures can be more difficult to draw than figures with straight sides, so it can be helpful to review the definitions of these figures when you have a need to create them. For a circle, any point on its curve is equidistant from the center, and this distance from the center, called the *radius*, would be the length of a string used to make the circle. Thus when you are making a circle, fasten one end of the string to the center point, tie the other end of the string to a pencil, and <u>sweep</u> completely around to draw the shape.

Another familiar curved figure is the ellipse. This egg-shaped figure appears to be very difficult to draw, but a review of the underlying definition provides the appropriate clue. An ellipse, like a circle, has a center point, but it also has two focus points (A and B). The definition says that the sum of lines such as AC and BC, which connect the focus points to the curve of the ellipse, must be constant no matter where the lines connect to the curve. To draw an ellipse, fasten a string to points A and B, as shown in the diagram. Stretch the string with a pencil to point C and sweep completely around, keeping the string tight as you proceed. You'll end up with an ellipse.

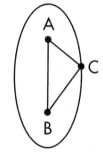

Main Idea   1

	Answer	Score
Mark the *main idea*	M	15
Mark the statement that is *too broad*	B	5
Mark the statement that is *too narrow*	N	5

a. An ellipse has two focus points. ☐ _____

b. Geometric shapes can all be drawn. ☐ _____

c. Understanding a definition can help you find a way to draw a geometric figure. ☐ _____

Subject Matter   **2**   Another good title for this passage would be
☐ a. Drawing Geometric Shapes.
☐ b. Writing Definitions for Geometric Shapes.
☐ c. Using Focus Points.
☐ d. Equations for Shapes in Geometry.   _____

Supporting Details   **3**   The distance from the center to a point on a circle is called the
☐ a. diameter.
☐ b. curve.
☐ c. focus point.
☐ d. radius.   _____

Conclusion   **4**   According to the descriptions in this passage,
☐ a. it is easier to draw a circle than an ellipse.
☐ b. it is easier to draw an ellipse than a circle.
☐ c. an ellipse can be either circular or oval.
☐ d. a piece of string should be used in drawing a rectangle.   _____

Clarifying Devices   **5**   The words in quotation marks in the first paragraph are
☐ a. statements made by mathematicians.
☐ b. instructions for drawing right angles.
☐ c. definitions.
☐ d. instructions for drawing circles.   _____

Vocabulary in Context   **6**   In this passage, the word <u>sweep</u> means
☐ a. move completely around.
☐ b. search thoroughly.
☐ c. clean or clear away.
☐ d. remove or erase.   _____

Add your scores for questions 1–6. Enter the total here and on the graph on page 160.   **Total Score**   _____

63 Zeno's Paradoxes

Paradoxes are statements that may be true but they express contradictory ideas. Some people find paradoxes enjoyable and thought-provoking while others find them frustrating, but most mathematicians would agree that these puzzling situations have played an important role in the history of philosophical thought.

Zeno of Elea (495–435 B.C.) was a Greek philosopher now best known for inventing several paradoxes that caused mathematicians to question the very nature of time and space. In one of Zeno's paradoxes, the fast-running Achilles and a tortoise run a race, but the tortoise is allowed a head start because he is so much slower than Achilles. Zeno contends that Achilles can't win the race because he must first reach the place from which the tortoise started. But when Achilles reaches that location, the tortoise has departed and therefore is ahead. The argument is repeated over and over, thereby proving that the more slowly moving tortoise is always ahead of Achilles.

In another paradox, Zeno demonstrates that any motion at all is actually impossible! To proceed from point A to point B, an object must first reach the middle of the distance; but before it reaches the middle, it must first reach the quarter mark; and so on. The object can never get from point A to point B; in fact, the motion can never even begin.

These types of paradoxes are usually explained by positing that both space and time are infinitely divisible; that is, the number of points on a line segment—or the number of instants in a time interval—has nothing to do with the length of the segment. However, since most of us are as perplexed by these infinite categories as by the original paradoxes themselves, Zeno's conundrums remain as intriguingly annoying as they have been for more than 2,000 years.

Main Idea	1		
		Answer	Score
	Mark the *main idea*	M	15
	Mark the statement that is *too broad*	B	5
	Mark the statement that is *too narrow*	N	5

a. Zeno's paradoxes challenged assumptions about space and time. ☐ ____

b. Paradoxes are statements that may be true but seem to say opposite things. ☐ ____

c. In one of Zeno's paradoxes, Achilles never passes the tortoise. ☐ ____

Score 15 points for each correct answer.   **Score**

Subject Matter   **2**   This passage is mainly about
☐ a. various kinds of infinite categories.
☐ b. the history of Greek philosophy.
☐ c. the meaning of paradox.
☐ d. two paradoxes involved with motion.   _____

Supporting Details   **3**   In the paradox about Achilles and the tortoise,
☐ a. the tortoise always wins.
☐ b. Achilles always wins.
☐ c. sometimes Achilles wins and sometimes the tortoise does.
☐ d. neither one wins.   _____

Conclusion   **4**   It is probably the case that Elea is or was a
☐ a. family of Greek philosophers.
☐ b. place in Greece.
☐ c. famous school of philosophers.
☐ d. Greek church or temple.   _____

Clarifying Devices   **5**   The writer of the passage describes two of Zeno's paradoxes
☐ a. and then refers to several others.
☐ b. and then proves they are false.
☐ c. but does not fully explain how they work.
☐ d. but then points out that they are no longer important.   _____

Vocabulary in Context   **6**   In this passage, the word <u>positing</u> means
☐ a. setting in a fixed position.
☐ b. proposing.
☐ c. denying.
☐ d. drawing a diagram of.   _____

Add your scores for questions 1–6. Enter the total here and on the graph on page 160.   **Total Score**   _____

64 A Creative Leap

Your own memories of algebra classes may contradict the notion of creativity. Perhaps you were unfortunate enough to be exposed only to lesson after lesson of mind-numbing drill. To gain an appreciation for the creative side of algebra, consider for a moment the supremely creative notion embedded in the familiar algebraic phrase, *Let* x *equal*.

To refresh your memory of how this phrase appears, consider a problem in which you are to find two consecutive integers, or whole numbers, with a sum of 35. The usual solution strategy is to begin by saying, "Let x equal the first integer and then $x + 1$ equals the second integer." The solution proceeds with the equation $x + (x + 1) = 35$. The solution, or x, is the smaller of the two integers, 17. That is, 17 plus 18 equals 35. The problem has been solved by letting x stand for the smaller unknown number.

This type of algebraic problem-solving is usually taught in such a humdrum manner that the surprising and creative part of the process is lost. The magic of the approach is that, faced with a seemingly incomprehensible problem about consecutive integers, a student is directed to take the optimistic leap that a solution has already been found! The idea of letting x equal the solution assumes two things. First, there exists a solution. And, second, the student can <u>forge</u> ahead, following the specified steps, and eventually reach the happy event of finding that solution. The creative part of algebra is not in the cleverness of the problem-solving strategies but rather in the wonderful and comforting notion that a solution always exists and that, somehow, you will be able to find it.

Main Idea	1			
			Answer	**Score**
	Mark the *main idea*		M	15
	Mark the statement that is *too broad*		B	5
	Mark the statement that is *too narrow*		N	5

a. Using the unknown x in algebra is an act of creativity.

b. Many algebraic solutions are extremely creative.

c. Problems about consecutive integers can be solved with algebraic equations.

Score 15 points for each correct answer.   **Score**

Subject Matter 2 This passage is mainly about
- [ ] a. problems about consecutive integers.
- [ ] b. increasing a person's creativity.
- [ ] c. the importance of drill problems in algebra.
- [ ] d. using the variable x to write equations.   _____

Supporting Details 3 The two consecutive integers that have a sum of 35 are
- [ ] a. 16 and 17.
- [ ] b. 17 and 17.
- [ ] c. 17 and 18.
- [ ] d. impossible to figure out without algebra.   _____

Conclusion 4 If a math problem asks you to find the time it takes to drive a distance, you could start by writing, Let x equal
- [ ] a. the distance in miles.
- [ ] b. the speed in miles per hour.
- [ ] c. the time in hours.
- [ ] d. two consecutive integers.   _____

Clarifying Devices 5 The writer of the passage conveys a fondness for algebra by
- [ ] a. showing you a way to solve a problem.
- [ ] b. emphasizing how creative it is.
- [ ] c. downplaying the importance of drill.
- [ ] d. describing practical uses for it.   _____

Vocabulary in Context 6 In this passage, the word <u>forge</u> means
- [ ] a. advance gradually but steadily.
- [ ] b. harden over a fire.
- [ ] c. form or create.
- [ ] d. fake a solution.   _____

Add your scores for questions 1–6. Enter the total here and on the graph on page 160.   **Total Score**   _____

65 What's Rational About That?

If you glance through the table of contents of a grammar school or high school mathematics textbook, you are likely to encounter the term *rational number*. While you are familiar with whole numbers, fractions, decimals, and percentages, you may well wonder what a rational number is and how you passed through your school mathematics classes without encountering one.

In fact, you did learn definitions and applications for rational numbers, although rational numbers may not have been identified as such in your classes. A rational number is any number that can be expressed as a ratio of two whole numbers, so $\frac{4}{5}$ (the ratio of 4 to 5), $\frac{2}{3}$ (ratio of 2 to 3), and in fact all fractions are members of the set of rational numbers. Also included are all terminating decimals such as 0.25 (equal to $\frac{1}{4}$ or 1 to 4) and repeating decimals like 0.333 . . . (equal to $\frac{1}{3}$ or 1 to 3). Percentages are rational numbers, too, as every percentage has an implied denominator of 100; for example, 35 percent equals the ratio 35 to 100, or 35 out of 100 parts. Even ordinary, everyday whole numbers are members of the set of rational numbers, since a whole number such as 4 can be written as $\frac{4}{1}$ or the ratio 4 to 1. So your math classes have involved work with all these types of rational numbers as you learned to compute, estimate, and solve problems with them.

This brief description of the major subsets of the rational numbers may give you the impression that *all* numbers are rational, but that is not the case. For example, the square root of the number 9 is 3, a rational number. But the square roots of numbers such as 5 and 10 do not equal whole numbers and cannot be expressed as ratios. Square roots that cannot be written as ratios are not rational numbers.

Main Idea	1		
		Answer	**Score**
	Mark the *main idea*	M	15
	Mark the statement that is *too broad*	B	5
	Mark the statement that is *too narrow*	N	5
	a. Not all square roots are rational numbers.	☐	____
	b. Many different types of numbers are studied in school math classes.	☐	____
	c. Rational numbers include all types of numbers that can be written as ratios.	☐	____

Score 15 points for each correct answer. **Score**

Subject Matter   **2**   This passage is mostly concerned with
    ☐ a. persuading you to like math.
    ☐ b. explaining problems that use ratios.
    ☐ c. the definition of the term *rational number.*
    ☐ d. describing how to find square roots.   _____

Supporting   **3**   The number .25 is an example of
Details
    ☐ a. a square root.
    ☐ b. an irrational number.
    ☐ c. a terminating decimal.
    ☐ d. a repeating decimal.   _____

Conclusion   **4**   When whole numbers are written as ratios, the
    second number in the ratio must always be
    ☐ a. 1.
    ☐ b. 0.
    ☐ c. larger than 1.
    ☐ d. a decimal.   _____

Clarifying   **5**   The passage explains what rational numbers are by
Devices
    ☐ a. defining categories of numbers.
    ☐ b. giving examples.
    ☐ c. proving theorems.
    ☐ d. showing examples that use computation.   _____

Vocabulary   **6**   In this passage, <u>implied</u> means
in Context
    ☐ a. not necessary.
    ☐ b. proven.
    ☐ c. made up of fractions.
    ☐ d. not stated directly.   _____

Add your scores for questions 1–6. Enter the total here   **Total**
and on the graph on page 160.   **Score**   _____

66 Precision and Common Sense

Consider the following anecdote and look for the mathematical misconception that underlies its humor. A small child who was looking at fossils in a museum asked a guard how old the fossils were. When the guard responded that they were 30 million and 8 years old, the child's skeptical parent asked where the age estimate came from. The guard answered that he had been working at the museum for eight years and had been told the fossils were 30 million years old when he started work.

The mathematical error embodied in the anecdote is that of misinterpreting the precision of the number 30 million. In the story, 30 million years was never intended as a precise time period, but rather should have been construed to mean "about 30 million years" or even "between 25 and 35 million years." The degree of imprecision is unknown from just the information given in the anecdote and could only be determined from locating the scientist who made the estimate.

If a number is the sum or product of other numbers, the precision of that number is much affected by the precision of its component parts. Let's say two people are measuring the length and width of a room to determine its area. If one person estimates the width visually as about 10 feet while the other person carefully measures to the nearest inch, an area computed in square inches would have a meaningless precision.

Thus, common sense should be used generously when interpreting numbers used as measurements or counts. Before accepting any number literally, pause and think about the accuracy with which the original measurement or estimation was worked out.

Main Idea	1	Answer	Score
	Mark the *main idea*	M	15
	Mark the statement that is *too broad*	B	5
	Mark the statement that is *too narrow*	N	5

a. Some numbers are more specific than others. ☐ _____

b. The age of any fossil is just an estimate. ☐ _____

c. It is important to describe or specify the precision of numbers used in scientific work. ☐ _____

Score 15 points for each correct answer.   **Score**

Subject Matter   **2**   Another good title for this passage would be
☐ a. 30,000,008 Years Old?
☐ b. Imprecise Numbers in Archaeology.
☐ c. Measuring the Ages of Fossils.
☐ d. Finding Areas by Measuring Lengths.   _____

Supporting Details   **3**   Using the number 30 million to describe the age of dinosaurs is very
☐ a. precise.
☐ b. imprecise.
☐ c. inaccurate.
☐ d. confusing.   _____

Conclusion   **4**   If you subtract a very imprecise number from one that is extremely precise, the answer will be
☐ a. a sum.
☐ b. given in square feet.
☐ c. very precise.
☐ d. very imprecise.   _____

Clarifying Devices   **5**   The purpose of the introductory paragraph is to
☐ a. show how uninformed museum workers can be.
☐ b. provide an example using simple arithmetic.
☐ c. introduce a concept by telling a story.
☐ d. give a clear definition of a million.   _____

Vocabulary in Context   **6**   In this passage, construed means
☐ a. recorded.
☐ b. understood.
☐ c. computed.
☐ d. measured.   _____

Add your scores for questions 1–6. Enter the total here and on the graph on page 160.   **Total Score**   _____

67 What's It Worth to You?

Perhaps you have made a major purchase recently, and the sales clerk asked if you wanted to purchase replacement insurance. This type of insurance is frequently offered for appliances and electronics. If you buy replacement insurance, you will receive a new item if your purchase breaks within some specified time period, such as the first year.

Is there some kind of mathematical principle you can use to decide whether you should buy this type of insurance, or must you simply guess whether your new purchase will break within the specified time period? As with many everyday problem-solving situations, mathematics can provide you with some assistance in your decision making. To determine whether you should purchase the replacement insurance, it is necessary to compute what statisticians call the *expected cost.* An example will serve to <u>illuminate</u> both the mathematical principle and the computations involved.

Suppose an item costs $60, and the insurance costs $20. You know that one-fourth of items of this type break during the insured period. Think about buying many of these items and needing to replace one-fourth of them. This would be the same as paying an additional one-fourth of $60, or $15, for each item.

The *expected cost* is defined as the cost of the item PLUS the average cost of replacing the item. The item costs $60; the replacement cost (on the average) is $15. Therefore, the expected cost is $60 + $15, or $75. Compare this expected cost to the cost of the item plus the cost of insurance ($60 + $20). Since $75 is less than $80, the replacement insurance is not a wise choice in this situation.

Main Idea	1		Answer	Score
	Mark the *main idea*		M	15
	Mark the statement that is *too broad*		B	5
	Mark the statement that is *too narrow*		N	5

a. Understanding insurance involves many mathematical applications. ☐ ____

b. Figuring expected cost helps in deciding if you need replacement insurance. ☐ ____

c. Expected cost is the sum of two quantities. ☐ ____

Score 15 points for each correct answer.   **Score**

Subject Matter   **2**   This passage is mostly concerned with figuring out
- ☐ a. the rising cost of insurance.
- ☐ b. how to get refunds for defective products.
- ☐ c. when you need replacement insurance.
- ☐ d. how to know whether a product will fail.   _____

Supporting   **3**   If you buy replacement insurance and your new
Details   purchase breaks down, you
- ☐ a. get your money back.
- ☐ b. get a new product exactly the same as the one that broke.
- ☐ c. can pick a new product of equal value.
- ☐ d. must purchase the insurance a second time.   _____

Supporting   **4**   If a product has a failure rate of one-fourth, then about
Details   what fraction of the items will fail or break within the
given time period?
- ☐ a. 25%
- ☐ b. $33\frac{1}{3}$%
- ☐ c. 50%
- ☐ d. 75%   _____

Clarifying   **5**   The passage explains expected cost by
Devices
- ☐ a. defining replacement insurance.
- ☐ b. explaining insurance probabilities.
- ☐ c. giving failure rates for various products.
- ☐ d. giving an example of how it works.   _____

Vocabulary   **6**   In this passage, the word <u>illuminate</u> means to
in Context
- ☐ a. decorate with candles.
- ☐ b. brighten with lights.
- ☐ c. make understandable.
- ☐ d. prove.   _____

Add your scores for questions 1–6. Enter the total here   **Total**
and on the graph on page 160.   **Score**   _____

68 A Visual Illusion

You probably imagine that you can visually distinguish straight lines and edges from curved lines using your experiences or instincts whether a line <u>veers</u> away from a perfect horizontal or vertical. Most people do possess a good sense of whether something is straight or curved, owing perhaps to a perceptive ability that we are all born with. But the distinction between straight and curved is not always as clearcut as it might seem. Your eyes and mind can be fooled into thinking that a curved line exists where in actuality there is only a set of straight lines.

The figure that accompanies this passage demonstrates one way to blur the distinction between what is straight and what is curved. The example construction is based on connecting numbered pairs of points in a specified manner—in this case, 12 straight lines are drawn, with the result that a curve approximating that of a quarter circle emerges. The 24 connected points are positioned at equal distances along the two sides of a right, or 90 degree, angle. By varying the size of the angle as well as the number and positioning of the points, a wide variety of interesting and attractive "curved" figures can be created from straight line segments.

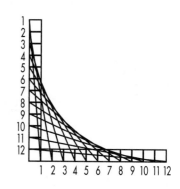

Main Idea	1 ———————————————		
		Answer	**Score**
	Mark the *main idea*	M	15
	Mark the statement that is *too broad*	B	5
	Mark the statement that is *too narrow*	N	5

a. Straight lines can be positioned to create the illusion of a curve.　☐　____

b. Many people are tricked by visual illusions.　☐　____

c. A right angle is used in creating one illusion of a curve.　☐　____

Score 15 points for each correct answer.   **Score**

Subject Matter   **2**   This passage is mainly about
☐ a. drawing lines within right angles.
☐ b. characteristics of curved lines.
☐ c. characteristics of straight lines.
☐ d. creating a specific type of visual illusion.   _____

Supporting Details   **3**   The curve in the diagram
☐ a. is actually made from 12 straight lines.
☐ b. can only be seen from a certain angle.
☐ c. contains 24 small line segments.
☐ d. creates a 90 degree angle.   _____

Conclusion   **4**   The final sentence of this passage suggests that by varying the size of the angle, you might be able to draw
☐ a. larger circles.
☐ b. part of an oval.
☐ c. various sizes of rectangles.
☐ d. longer straight lines.   _____

Clarifying Devices   **5**   The points along the sides of the angle are numbered to
☐ a. prove there are more than 10 points on each side of the angle.
☐ b. show that the angle has 90 degrees.
☐ c. demonstrate how to connect them.
☐ d. make the figure look like a graph.   _____

Vocabulary in Context   **6**   In this passage, <u>veers</u> means
☐ a. moves away from.
☐ b. becomes parallel with.
☐ c. zigzags.
☐ d. continues without ending.   _____

Add your scores for questions 1–6. Enter the total here and on the graph on page 160.   **Total Score**   _____

69 Equilateral and Equiangular

From the standpoint of aesthetic appeal, no class of geometric figures can compare with the regular polygons. These rotationally symmetric shapes have such a satisfying completeness that they have found extensive applications in all the visual arts.

The first, or simplest, of the regular polygons is that with the least number of sides, the equilateral triangle. You have observed this shape in yield signs from the window of a moving car, as well as in other types of informational or cautionary signs. This three-sided exemplar of the class of regular polygons <u>evidences</u> the distinctive characteristics of the group—to be designated "regular," a polygon must possess sides and angles of equal dimension. It is not sufficient to have just all equal sides or all equal angles, as shown by the four-sided rhombus, a polygon with four equal sides but lacking the necessary four equal angles (two sides are diagonal). Thus a rhombus is not regular. The four-sided polygon that does have this distinction is the familiar square.

Perhaps the most convenient method of constructing regular polygons involves using the central angles of a circle. To illustrate the procedure to be followed, consider the regular pentagon, the equilateral and equiangular polygon with five sides. Draw any circle, mark the center point, and divide the total central angle measure of 360 degrees by 5 to get 72. Using a protractor, divide the circle into five equal sectors, each with a central angle of 72 degrees. By connecting the points on the rim of the circle, you will have—subject to the accuracy of your construction techniques—a perfect regular pentagon. Using this construction approach, you may enjoy creating for yourself regular polygons with six sides (hexagons), seven sides (heptagons), eight sides (octagons), and so forth. One caution: if your intent is to create a regular figure with a large number of sides, be sure to begin your drawing activity with a very large circle!

Main Idea   1

	Answer	Score
Mark the *main idea*	M	15
Mark the statement that is *too broad*	B	5
Mark the statement that is *too narrow*	N	5

a. To construct a regular polygon with 5 sides, first divide 360 degrees by 5. ☐ _____

b. A few geometric figures are regular polygons. ☐ _____

c. Regular polygons are visually pleasing and easy to construct with central angles. ☐ _____

Subject Matter　　**2**　This passage is mainly about
- ☐ a. measuring angles.
- ☐ b. flat shapes with all equal sides and angles.
- ☐ c. triangles with three equal sides.
- ☐ d. names for different kinds of polygons.　　＿＿

Supporting Details　　**3**　The angles of a rhombus are
- ☐ a. less than 90 degrees.
- ☐ b. more than 90 degrees.
- ☐ c. all the same size.
- ☐ d. not all the same size.　　＿＿

Conclusion　　**4**　A protractor is a tool used to
- ☐ a. measure and draw angles.
- ☐ b. measure circles.
- ☐ c. draw straight line segments.
- ☐ d. draw equilateral triangles.　　＿＿

Clarifying Devices　　**5**　The parentheses in this passage are used for
- ☐ a. definitions.
- ☐ b. information unrelated to the topic.
- ☐ c. explanatory notes.
- ☐ d. side comments by the writer.　　＿＿

Vocabulary in Context　　**6**　In this passage, the word <u>evidences</u> means
- ☐ a. surprises.
- ☐ b. denies.
- ☐ c. shows clearly.
- ☐ d. contradicts.　　＿＿

Add your scores for questions 1–6. Enter the total here and on the graph on page 160.　　Total Score　＿＿

70 Looking Across for Answers

Imagine you are unfortunate enough to be caught in a traffic <u>snarl</u> with the effect that you and your vehicle progress only 45 miles in two entire hours! At this average rate of speed, it will take a total of four hours to cover 90 miles; that is, 45 miles in 2 hours is the same rate as 90 miles in 4 hours.

The equivalency of these two rates is illustrated by the mathematical expression displayed in the box. This is one practical application of using two equal rates to form a proportion. An attribute or property of all proportions that is immensely useful is that the two cross products are of necessity equal. In this example, the two cross products are 45 times 4 and 2 times 90, each pair of factors being diagonally opposite or across from each other.

$$\frac{45 \text{ miles}}{2 \text{ hours}} = \frac{90 \text{ miles}}{4 \text{ hours}}$$

The equivalency of cross products is useful because it allows you to solve for a missing term in a proportional expression. To continue with our traffic snarl example, suppose you wish to know how far you may expect to travel in $3\frac{1}{2}$ hours. Set up your proportion using the fractions $\frac{45}{2}$ and $\frac{N}{3.5}$, multiply to find the cross-products, and then solve the resulting simple equation for N. In a like manner, the time required to travel any given distance at this very slow rate of speed can be determined.

This useful cross-product strategy can be applied in the solution of a wide variety of practical applications—almost any situation, in fact, that involves rates, ratios, speeds, and measurement conversions.

Main Idea   1

	Answer	Score
Mark the *main idea*	M	15
Mark the statement that is *too broad*	B	5
Mark the statement that is *too narrow*	N	5

a. Forty-five miles in two hours is equivalent to 90 in four hours. ☐ _____

b. Solving mathematical problems involves an understanding of basic properties. ☐ _____

c. A key property of proportions is that the cross products are equal. ☐ _____

Score 15 points for each correct answer.   Score

Subject Matter 2 This passage is primarily concerned with
☐ a. finding average speeds.
☐ b. mathematical qualities of speed.
☐ c. understanding fractions.
☐ d. proportions and how to solve them.   _____

Supporting Details 3 The example in the box uses two equal rates to show
☐ a. a ratio.
☐ b. an average distance.
☐ c. an attribute.
☐ d. a proportion.   _____

Conclusion 4 The cross products for the proportion
$\frac{45}{2} = \frac{N}{3.5}$ are
☐ a. 45 times 3.5; 2 times N.
☐ b. 45 times 2; N times 3.5.
☐ c. 45 times N; 2 times 3.5.
☐ d. not equal.   _____

Clarifying Devices 5 The real-world example of proportion used in the passage involves figuring out
☐ a. distance.
☐ b. time.
☐ c. speed.
☐ d. acceleration.   _____

Vocabulary in Context 6 In this passage, the word <u>snarl</u> means a
☐ a. vicious growl.
☐ b. tangled situation.
☐ c. dangerous situation.
☐ d. confusing situation.   _____

Add your scores for questions 1–6. Enter the total here and on the graph on page 160.   Total Score   _____

71 Only Length Times Width?

Once they have finished their last math course, most people think of the concept of "area" only in the context of rectangular regions. They may compare sizes of houses in square feet or check the coverage abilities of paint in square yards. Since the majority of area applications seem to involve rectangles, it is not surprising that many people think of area as being only the result of multiplying the length of a figure times its width.

Thinking of area only in terms of this formula is quite limiting, however, as the majority of shapes are more complicated than rectangles. In fact, area is a much broader concept than a simple formula. It embodies the notion of a surface covering. In the same way that a length is quantified by relating it to standard linear units such as inches, area is measured in standard square units. The most <u>tangible</u> way of demonstrating area is to use a set of one-inch tiles and have the learner cover, or approximately cover, a flat object such as a drawing of a lamp with the tiles. This exercise emphasizes the fact that almost all areas are approximations and that "multiply the length times the width" applies only to determining areas of rectangles and squares.

Of course many geometric figures *do* have area formulas, and these are quite useful in situations where triangles, trapezoids, parallelograms, and their like are involved in problem-solving exercises. But remembering the underlying concept that an area is a covering of standard square units allows you to find the area of *any* shape, no matter how irregular. You can place a transparent square grid over the shape and then count or estimate the number of square units that cover the interior.

Main Idea   1

	Answer	Score
Mark the *main idea*	M	15
Mark the statement that is *too broad*	B	5
Mark the statement that is *too narrow*	N	5

a. The important idea about area is that it is a region covered by square units. ☐ _____

b. Figures like triangles and trapezoids use various area formulas. ☐ _____

c. Mathematics involves concepts as well as formulas. ☐ _____

Score 15 points for each correct answer. Score

Subject Matter 2 This passage primarily helps the reader to
☐ a. learn to differentiate area from perimeter.
☐ b. think of area as a covering rather than the answer to a formula.
☐ c. stop using area formulas.
☐ d. see that area is an important math topic. _____

Supporting Details 3 Multiplying length times width gives the area of
☐ a. a trapezoid.
☐ b. a parallelogram.
☐ c. a rectangle.
☐ d. any geometric figure. _____

Conclusion 4 A transparent square grid would be a particularly useful tool to find the area of
☐ a. a very large shape.
☐ b. a very small shape.
☐ c. any shape with four sides.
☐ d. an irregular shape. _____

Clarifying Devices 5 The use of one-inch square tiles is described as helpful for
☐ a. helping learners understand the basic concept of area.
☐ b. finding areas of shapes like triangles.
☐ c. teaching learners how to draw a grid.
☐ d. connecting area and linear measurements. _____

Vocabulary in Context 6 In this passage, the word <u>tangible</u> means
☐ a. made out of a touchable substance.
☐ b. valuable.
☐ c. clear and obvious.
☐ d. practical. _____

Add your scores for questions 1–6. Enter the total here and on the graph on page 160. Total Score _____

72 Making Patterns with Numbers

The numbers 1, 3, 6, and 10 can be shown as dots in triangles, so they are called *triangular numbers*. In each triangle, there is 1 dot in the top row, 2 dots in the next row, and then 3 dots, 4 dots, and so on.

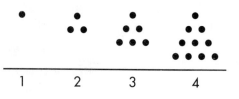

Triangular numbers demonstrate connections between geometry and arithmetic. A geometry idea is shown in the name *triangular numbers*. You can see an arithmetic idea if you write sums of consecutive integers:

$$1=1 \qquad 1+2=3 \qquad 1+2+3=6 \qquad 1+2+3+4=10$$

The next sums will be 1 through 5, 1 through 6, and 1 through 7, so the next three triangular numbers will be 15, 21, and 28.

You can see a link between square numbers and arithmetic if you add series of consecutive odd integers:

$$1=1 \qquad 1+3=4 \qquad 1+3+5=9 \qquad 1+3+5+7=16 \qquad 1+3+5+7+9=25$$

Those sums are the square numbers!

Numbers that can be shown as familiar shapes are called *figurate numbers*. The triangular numbers 1, 3, 6, and 10 are figurate numbers, and so are the numbers 1, 4, 9, 16, 25, and so on. These numbers can be represented by squares, where the number of dots on the sides of the squares are 1, 2, 3, and so on.

Figurate numbers contain many interesting relationships for the curious to uncover. For example, try adding adjacent, or bordering, pairs of triangular numbers (1+3 or 3+6). Do you see a familiar pattern beginning to show?

Main Idea	1		
		Answer	**Score**
	Mark the *main idea*	M	15
	Mark the statement that is *too broad*	B	5
	Mark the statement that is *too narrow*	N	5

a. Square and triangular numbers are two kinds of figurate numbers. ☐ _____

b. The fourth triangular number is 10. ☐ _____

c. Number patterns can be interesting and surprising. ☐ _____

Subject Matter   2   This passage is mostly concerned with
☐ a. applications of triangles and squares.
☐ b. numbers that can be shown with geometric
  arrangements of dots.
☐ c. finding squares of numbers.
☐ d. finding sums of number sequences.   _____

Supporting   3   The third triangular number is
Details   ☐ a. 3.
☐ b. 6.
☐ c. 10.
☐ d. 15.   _____

Conclusion   4   Adding bordering pairs of triangular numbers
creates a sequence of
☐ a. square numbers.
☐ b. odd numbers.
☐ c. even numbers.
☐ d. fractions.   _____

Clarifying   5   The illustration shows that the fourth triangular
Devices   number is the sum of
☐ a. 1 + 3 + 5.
☐ b. 1 + 3 + 5 + 7.
☐ c. 1 + 2 + 3.
☐ d. 1 + 2 + 3 + 4.   _____

Vocabulary   6   In this passage, the word <u>consecutive</u> means
in Context   ☐ a. added to other numbers.
☐ b. not equal.
☐ c. following one another in order.
☐ d. complimentary.   _____

Add your scores for questions 1–6. Enter the total here   **Total**
and on the graph on page 160.   **Score**   _____

73 The Impossible Equation

Introductory algebra deals with the solutions of various types of equations, some simple and others quite complex. Each solution of an equation is a number that, when substituted into the equation, results in a true statement. Some equations have more than one solution. For example, $x^2 - 5x + 6 = 0$ is solved by substituting either the number 2 or the number 3 for the letter variable x.

In the history of mathematics, one seemingly simple equation must have caused tremendous frustration for mathematicians. On the one hand, it appeared so <u>trivial</u>; on the other hand, no one could find a whole number or a fractional number for a solution. The annoyingly simple equation is $x^2 + 1 = 0$. Some brief experimentation should convince you that no number of the ordinary sort will make this equation true.

What kind of number, if any, can be thought of as the solution to $x^2 + 1 = 0$? Years ago, some mathematicians preferred to say that equations of this type had no solution; they were said to be "absurd." Solutions of these equations were called meaningless or impossible or imaginary. Other mathematicians felt that $x^2 + 1 = 0$ and the related set of equations $x^2 + a = 0$, where a is greater than 0, had to have some kind of solution. It was proposed to just *define* a solution, and the imaginary number i was eventually accepted to equal the square root of negative 1. Squaring i gives negative 1 and so the solution to $x^2 + 1 = 0$ is the imaginary number i, a member of a larger set called the complex numbers that take the form $a + bi$.

Imaginary and complex numbers should not be thought of as being without reality—they obey the standard laws of arithmetic, and they are just as real, in their own way, as familiar everyday whole numbers.

Main Idea   1 ——————————————————————————

	Answer	Score
Mark the *main idea*	M	15
Mark the statement that is *too broad*	B	5
Mark the statement that is *too narrow*	N	5

a. Imaginary and complex numbers are advanced mathematical concepts. ☐ ____

b. The equation $x^2 + 1 = 0$ has no immediately obvious solution. ☐ ____

c. Imaginary numbers were invented to solve equations of the form $x^2 + a = 0$. ☐ ____

Score 15 points for each correct answer.   **Score**

Subject Matter   **2** This passage is mainly about
- ☐ a. ways to solve equations.
- ☐ b. the invention of imaginary numbers.
- ☐ c. equations that have no reality.
- ☐ d. the development of difficult equations.   _____

Supporting   **3** Equations like $x^2 + 1 = 0$ were called "absurd" since
Details
- ☐ a. no ordinary sort of number could solve them.
- ☐ b. it was a waste of time to work with them.
- ☐ c. there were thousands of possible solutions.
- ☐ d. there were three or four solutions, but all were silly.   _____

Conclusion   **4** The passage implies that finding solutions to equations
- ☐ a. is a very important issue for mathematicians.
- ☐ b. is usually difficult or impossible.
- ☐ c. always involves using imaginary and complex numbers.
- ☐ d. is too elementary for most mathematicians.   _____

Clarifying   **5** The equation $x^2 - 5x + 6 = 0$ is given as an
Devices   example of an equation
- ☐ a. that cannot be solved.
- ☐ b. that can be solved.
- ☐ c. with only one possible solution.
- ☐ d. requiring the use of imaginary numbers.   _____

Vocabulary   **6** In this passage, the word <u>trivial</u> means
in Context
- ☐ a. always equal to zero.
- ☐ b. the simplest possible example.
- ☐ c. of little significance or value.
- ☐ d. unusual.   _____

Add your scores for questions 1–6. Enter the total here   **Total**
and on the graph on page 160.   **Score**   _____

74 Just Rolling Along

Here is a thought experiment to test your spatial visualization skills. Imagine a wheel with a red spot painted on its rim. Trace the path followed by the red spot as the wheel moves along. This path, which is shown below, creates a curve. This curve, well-known and much studied since the time of Galileo in the 1600s, is called a cycloid. It has a variety of interesting properties.

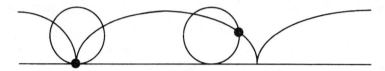

If you found it difficult to think about a moving spot, try a different experiment. Attach a marking pen to a bicycle wheel so that the pen is perpendicular to the wheel. Now roll the wheel along next to a piece of paper. As the wheel rolls forward, the pen will trace the loops, or arches, of the cycloid for you.

The cycloid is a curve with both practical and abstract properties. The opening to a tunnel or the arch of a bridge often takes this shape because a cycloid is the strongest shape for a curve. Mathematicians know that if they draw a square around one of the circles in the diagram above, the perimeter of that square will match the length of one complete arch of the cycloid.

Can a cycloid be represented by a mathematical equation? Yes, but the equation is complicated. The complexity of the cycloid's equation, however, need not prevent you from appreciating the cycloid's <u>aesthetic</u> appeal or from reading more about the role that the cycloid has played in the history of mathematics.

Main Idea	1		Answer	Score
	Mark the *main idea*		M	15
	Mark the statement that is *too broad*		B	5
	Mark the statement that is *too narrow*		N	5

a. Many mathematical curves are attractive in appearance. ☐ ____

b. The cycloid can be used as the shape of an arch. ☐ ____

c. The cycloid, generated by a point on a rolling circle, has a variety of properties. ☐ ____

Score 15 points for each correct answer.   **Score**

Subject Matter   **2**   This passage is mostly concerned with

☐ a. the properties of all algebraic curves.

☐ b. the properties of a certain type of
     mathematical curve.

☐ c. geometrical oddities shown by curves.

☐ d. figuring out the equation of the cycloid.   _____

Supporting   **3**   The black dots in the illustration show
Details

☐ a. a point on a turning wheel.

☐ b. the path of a bouncing ball.

☐ c. two bicycle wheels.

☐ d. two solutions to a cycloid equation.   _____

Conclusion   **4**   It is reasonable to assume from the passage that

☐ a. cycloids were discovered only recently.

☐ b. you cannot construct an arch unless you
     use a cycloid.

☐ c. many curves can be generated by points
     that move in different ways.

☐ d. the cycloid can only be drawn with a
     bicycle wheel.   _____

Clarifying   **5**   The passage, shows how a cycloid is formed by
Devices

☐ a. using an illustration.

☐ b. giving a verbal description.

☐ c. using an illustration and a verbal description.

☐ d. comparing it to more familiar kinds of curves.   _____

Vocabulary   **6**   In this passage, the word <u>aesthetic</u> means
in Context

☐ a. practical or down to earth.

☐ b. emotional.

☐ c. intellectual.

☐ d. artistic or beautiful.   _____

Add your scores for questions 1–6. Enter the total here   **Total**
and on the graph on page 160.   **Score**   _____

75 Putting the Pieces Together

An entire category of mathematical re-creations involves dissection puzzles, those tantalizing and sometimes infuriating activities in which you must cut one figure into pieces in order to transform it into something else. As a very simple example, a puzzle might involve transforming a square into a triangle by cutting the square into two pieces along the diagonal. In most dissection puzzles, the number of cuts is specified but determining their location is part of the problem left to the puzzler.

In the illustration is a Greek cross with a shaded "hole" the same size as one of the five squares that, taken together, create this type of cross. The dissection puzzle is to cut the cross into four parts so that the parts can be reassembled into a square. The solution shown is fairly simple once you know it—extend each side of the shaded square until you meet a vertex, or corner, of the cross. Then arrange the four pieces as shown in the final diagram of the illustration. The solution reveals the fact that the location of the square hole in the cross is by no means random, as its position and <u>orientation</u> must be such that the extensions of its sides meet the appropriate vertices.

Dissection puzzles similar to this one can be found in books of mathematical re-creations. They provide hours of enjoyment and help people sharpen their visual thinking skills. If this small taste of dissecting intrigues you, you may well become quite addicted to solving and perhaps even creating puzzles of this type.

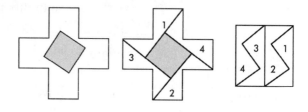

Main Idea	1		
		Answer	**Score**
	Mark the *main idea*	**M**	15
	Mark the statement that is *too broad*	**B**	5
	Mark the statement that is *too narrow*	**N**	5

a. A dissection puzzle involves cutting something into parts and then reassembling the parts. ☐ _____

b. Squares can be reassembled as triangles. ☐ _____

c. Solving geometrical puzzles can be quite addictive. ☐ _____

Score 15 points for each correct answer.   **Score**

Subject Matter 2 Another good title for this passage would be
  ☐ a. Cutting Shapes into Four Parts.
  ☐ b. Transforming a Cross.
  ☐ c. Properties of Cross-Shaped Figures.
  ☐ d. Creating Your Own Dissection Puzzles.   _____

Supporting Details 3 The solution to the Greek cross puzzle is a
  ☐ a. square made of four pieces.
  ☐ b. square made of two triangles.
  ☐ c. Greek cross without a hole in it.
  ☐ d. Greek cross with four numbered sections.   _____

Conclusion 4 Solving dissection puzzles like those described in the passage requires a high degree of
  ☐ a. manual dexterity.
  ☐ b. algebraic thinking.
  ☐ c. visual thinking.
  ☐ d. ability to follow the steps in a process.   _____

Clarifying Devices 5 A good way to better understand the first dissection puzzle described in the passage is to
  ☐ a. look up the definitions of some words.
  ☐ b. ask someone to solve the puzzle for you.
  ☐ c. skim the remaining part of the passage.
  ☐ d. make a drawing or sketch of the puzzle.   _____

Vocabulary in Context 6 In this passage, <u>orientation</u> means
  ☐ a. side length.
  ☐ b. area.
  ☐ c. angle.
  ☐ d. perimeter.   _____

Add your scores for questions 1–6. Enter the total here and on the graph on page 160.   **Total Score**   _____

Answer Key: Passages 1–25

Passage 1:	1a. N	1b. M	1c. B	2. b	3. d	4. b	5. a	6. b
Passage 2:	1a. M	1b. B	1c. N	2. c	3. d	4. b	5. d	6. c
Passage 3:	1a. N	1b. B	1c. M	2. b	3. c	4. a	5. c	6. a
Passage 4:	1a. N	1b. M	1c. B	2. a	3. c	4. d	5. b	6. b
Passage 5:	1a. N	1b. B	1c. M	2. c	3. a	4. b	5. b	6. d
Passage 6:	1a. N	1b. M	1c. B	2. c	3. c	4. c	5. d	6. c
Passage 7:	1a. M	1b. N	1c. B	2. b	3. d	4. a	5. c	6. b
Passage 8:	1a. B	1b. N	1c. M	2. a	3. c	4. c	5. b	6. d
Passage 9:	1a. M	1b. B	1c. N	2. c	3. a	4. a	5. b	6. c
Passage 10:	1a. M	1b. N	1c. B	2. d	3. b	4. a	5. c	6. a
Passage 11:	1a. N	1b. M	1c. B	2. c	3. b	4. c	5. d	6. a
Passage 12:	1a. M	1b. B	1c. N	2. b	3. d	4. c	5. a	6. b
Passage 13:	1a. N	1b. B	1c. M	2. b	3. c	4. d	5. a	6. c
Passage 14:	1a. M	1b. N	1c. B	2. b	3. c	4. d	5. c	6. a
Passage 15:	1a. N	1b. B	1c. M	2. a	3. d	4. b	5. b	6. c
Passage 16:	1a. M	1b. B	1c. N	2. b	3. d	4. d	5. d	6. a
Passage 17:	1a. M	1b. N	1c. B	2. b	3. d	4. c	5. a	6. b
Passage 18:	1a. B	1b. N	1c. M	2. c	3. b	4. a	5. a	6. d
Passage 19:	1a. M	1b. N	1c. B	2. c	3. d	4. b	5. a	6. c
Passage 20:	1a. B	1b. M	1c. N	2. c	3. b	4. b	5. c	6. a
Passage 21:	1a. N	1b. B	1c. M	2. b	3. d	4. c	5. a	6. c
Passage 22:	1a. N	1b. M	1c. B	2. c	3. b	4. a	5. b	6. a
Passage 23:	1a. B	1b. M	1c. N	2. b	3. c	4. a	5. a	6. c
Passage 24:	1a. M	1b. N	1c. B	2. d	3. b	4. a	5. b	6. b
Passage 25:	1a. N	1b. B	1c. N	2. b	3. d	4. b	5. b	6. c

Answer Key: Passages 26–50

Passage 26:	1a. **M**	1b. **B**	1c. **N**	2. **d**	3. **b**	4. **a**	5. **c**	6. **c**
Passage 27:	1a. **N**	1b. **M**	1c. **B**	2. **d**	3. **a**	4. **b**	5. **a**	6. **b**
Passage 28:	1a. **N**	1b. **B**	1c. **M**	2. **a**	3. **c**	4. **b**	5. **d**	6. **c**
Passage 29:	1a. **M**	1b. **N**	1c. **B**	2. **d**	3. **c**	4. **c**	5. **a**	6. **b**
Passage 30:	1a. **M**	1b. **B**	1c. **N**	2. **a**	3. **c**	4. **d**	5. **c**	6. **c**
Passage 31:	1a. **N**	1b. **B**	1c. **M**	2. **c**	3. **d**	4. **a**	5. **c**	6. **b**
Passage 32:	1a. **N**	1b. **M**	1c. **B**	2. **d**	3. **b**	4. **b**	5. **a**	6. **c**
Passage 33:	1a. **B**	1b. **M**	1c. **N**	2. **c**	3. **b**	4. **a**	5. **c**	6. **a**
Passage 34:	1a. **N**	1b. **B**	1c. **M**	2. **b**	3. **d**	4. **c**	5. **a**	6. **a**
Passage 35:	1a. **M**	1b. **B**	1c. **N**	2. **c**	3. **d**	4. **a**	5. **b**	6. **c**
Passage 36:	1a. **B**	1b. **M**	1c. **N**	2. **c**	3. **b**	4. **b**	5. **c**	6. **b**
Passage 37:	1a. **B**	1b. **M**	1c. **N**	2. **a**	3. **c**	4. **c**	5. **b**	6. **d**
Passage 38:	1a. **M**	1b. **B**	1c. **N**	2. **d**	3. **a**	4. **a**	5. **b**	6. **c**
Passage 39:	1a. **M**	1b. **N**	1c. **B**	2. **b**	3. **c**	4. **a**	5. **b**	6. **d**
Passage 40:	1a. **B**	1b. **N**	1c. **M**	2. **d**	3. **c**	4. **d**	5. **b**	6. **a**
Passage 41:	1a. **B**	1b. **M**	1c. **N**	2. **c**	3. **d**	4. **d**	5. **d**	6. **a**
Passage 42:	1a. **N**	1b. **M**	1c. **B**	2. **a**	3. **b**	4. **a**	5. **b**	6. **a**
Passage 43:	1a. **B**	1b. **N**	1c. **M**	2. **a**	3. **b**	4. **a**	5. **a**	6. **b**
Passage 44:	1a. **N**	1b. **B**	1c. **M**	2. **a**	3. **b**	4. **a**	5. **a**	6. **b**
Passage 45:	1a. **M**	1b. **N**	1c. **B**	2. **b**	3. **c**	4. **a**	5. **a**	6. **c**
Passage 46:	1a. **N**	1b. **M**	1c. **B**	2. **a**	3. **b**	4. **d**	5. **c**	6. **c**
Passage 47:	1a. **M**	1b. **N**	1c. **B**	2. **b**	3. **c**	4. **d**	5. **b**	6. **b**
Passage 48:	1a. **M**	1b. **B**	1c. **N**	2. **c**	3. **c**	4. **d**	5. **a**	6. **c**
Passage 49:	1a. **N**	1b. **M**	1c. **B**	2. **c**	3. **d**	4. **a**	5. **c**	6. **b**
Passage 50:	1a. **B**	1b. **N**	1c. **M**	2. **d**	3. **d**	4. **c**	5. **b**	6. **b**

Passage 51:	1a. **N**	1b. **M**	1c. **B**	2. **b**	3. **c**	4. **a**	5. **d**	6. **c**
Passage 52:	1a. **B**	1b. **N**	1c. **M**	2. **c**	3. **c**	4. **a**	5. **b**	6. **b**
Passage 53:	1a. **B**	1b. **N**	1c. **M**	2. **b**	3. **d**	4. **a**	5. **b**	6. **c**
Passage 54:	1a. **B**	1b. **N**	1c. **M**	2. **c**	3. **a**	4. **c**	5. **d**	6. **d**
Passage 55:	1a. **N**	1b. **B**	1c. **M**	2. **c**	3. **d**	4. **d**	5. **a**	6. **b**
Passage 56:	1a. **M**	1b. **B**	1c. **N**	2. **d**	3. **c**	4. **c**	5. **b**	6. **a**
Passage 57:	1a. **B**	1b. **M**	1c. **N**	2. **b**	3. **d**	4. **a**	5. **c**	6. **b**
Passage 58:	1a. **B**	1b. **N**	1c. **M**	2. **d**	3. **c**	4. **d**	5. **c**	6. **c**
Passage 59:	1a. **M**	1b. **B**	1c. **N**	2. **c**	3. **d**	4. **a**	5. **b**	6. **a**
Passage 60:	1a. **N**	1b. **M**	1c. **B**	2. **c**	3. **b**	4. **b**	5. **d**	6. **c**
Passage 61:	1a. **M**	1b. **B**	1c. **N**	2. **c**	3. **c**	4. **a**	5. **a**	6. **c**
Passage 62:	1a. **N**	1b. **B**	1c. **M**	2. **a**	3. **d**	4. **a**	5. **c**	6. **a**
Passage 63:	1a. **M**	1b. **B**	1c. **N**	2. **d**	3. **a**	4. **b**	5. **c**	6. **b**
Passage 64:	1a. **M**	1b. **B**	1c. **N**	2. **d**	3. **c**	4. **c**	5. **b**	6. **a**
Passage 65:	1a. **N**	1b. **B**	1c. **M**	2. **c**	3. **c**	4. **a**	5. **b**	6. **d**
Passage 66:	1a. **B**	1b. **N**	1c. **M**	2. **a**	3. **b**	4. **d**	5. **c**	6. **b**
Passage 67:	1a. **B**	1b. **M**	1c. **N**	2. **c**	3. **b**	4. **a**	5. **d**	6. **c**
Passage 68:	1a. **M**	1b. **B**	1c. **N**	2. **d**	3. **a**	4. **b**	5. **c**	6. **a**
Passage 69:	1a. **N**	1b. **B**	1c. **M**	2. **b**	3. **d**	4. **a**	5. **c**	6. **c**
Passage 70:	1a. **N**	1b. **B**	1c. **M**	2. **d**	3. **d**	4. **a**	5. **a**	6. **b**
Passage 71:	1a. **M**	1b. **N**	1c. **B**	2. **b**	3. **c**	4. **d**	5. **a**	6. **c**
Passage 72:	1a. **M**	1b. **N**	1c. **B**	2. **b**	3. **b**	4. **a**	5. **d**	6. **c**
Passage 73:	1a. **B**	1b. **N**	1c. **M**	2. **b**	3. **a**	4. **a**	5. **b**	6. **c**
Passage 74:	1a. **B**	1b. **N**	1c. **M**	2. **b**	3. **a**	4. **c**	5. **c**	6. **d**
Passage 75:	1a. **M**	1b. **N**	1c. **B**	2. **b**	3. **a**	4. **c**	5. **d**	6. **c**

Diagnostic Chart: Passages 1–25

Directions: For each passage, write your answers to the left of the dotted line in the blocks for each skill category. Then correct your answers using the Answer Key on page 152. If your answer is correct, do not make any more marks in the block. If your answer is incorrect, write the letter of the correct answer to the right of the dotted line.

	Categories of Comprehension Skills								
	1 Main Idea			2	3	4	5	6	
	Statement a	Statement b	Statement c	Subject Matter	Supporting Details	Conclusion	Clarifying Devices	Vocabulary in Context	
Passage 1									
Passage 2									
Passage 3									
Passage 4									
Passage 5									
Passage 6									
Passage 7									
Passage 8									
Passage 9									
Passage 10									
Passage 11									
Passage 12									
Passage 13									
Passage 14									
Passage 15									
Passage 16									
Passage 17									
Passage 18									
Passage 19									
Passage 20									
Passage 21									
Passage 22									
Passage 23									
Passage 24									
Passage 25									

Diagnostic Chart: Passages 26–50

Directions: For each passage, write your answers to the left of the dotted line in the blocks for each skill category. Then correct your answers using the Answer Key on page 153. If your answer is correct, do not make any more marks in the block. If your answer is incorrect, write the letter of the correct answer to the right of the dotted line.

	Categories of Comprehension Skills								
	1 Main Idea				2	3	4	5	6
	Statement a	Statement b	Statement c	Subject Matter	Supporting Details	Conclusion	Clarifying Devices	Vocabulary in Context	
Passage 26									
Passage 27									
Passage 28									
Passage 29									
Passage 30									
Passage 31									
Passage 32									
Passage 33									
Passage 34									
Passage 35									
Passage 36									
Passage 37									
Passage 38									
Passage 39									
Passage 40									
Passage 41									
Passage 42									
Passage 43									
Passage 44									
Passage 45									
Passage 46									
Passage 47									
Passage 48									
Passage 49									
Passage 50									

Diagnostic Chart: Passages 51–75

Directions: For each passage, write your answers to the left of the dotted line in the blocks for each skill category. Then correct your answers using the Answer Key on page 154. If your answer is correct, do not make any more marks in the block. If your answer is incorrect, write the letter of the correct answer to the right of the dotted line.

| | Categories of Comprehension Skills | | | | | | | | |
| | 1 Main Idea | | | 2 | 3 | 4 | 5 | 6 | |
	Statement a	Statement b	Statement c	Subject Matter	Supporting Details	Conclusion	Clarifying Devices	Vocabulary in Context	
Passage 51									
Passage 52									
Passage 53									
Passage 54									
Passage 55									
Passage 56									
Passage 57									
Passage 58									
Passage 59									
Passage 60									
Passage 61									
Passage 62									
Passage 63									
Passage 64									
Passage 65									
Passage 66									
Passage 67									
Passage 68									
Passage 69									
Passage 70									
Passage 71									
Passage 72									
Passage 73									
Passage 74									
Passage 75									

Progress Graph: Passages 1–25

Directions: Write your Total Score for each passage in the comprehension score box under the number of the passage. Then plot your score on the graph itself by putting a small *x* on the line directly above the number of the passage, across from the score you got for that passage. As you mark your score for each passage, graph your progress by drawing a line to connect the *x*'s.

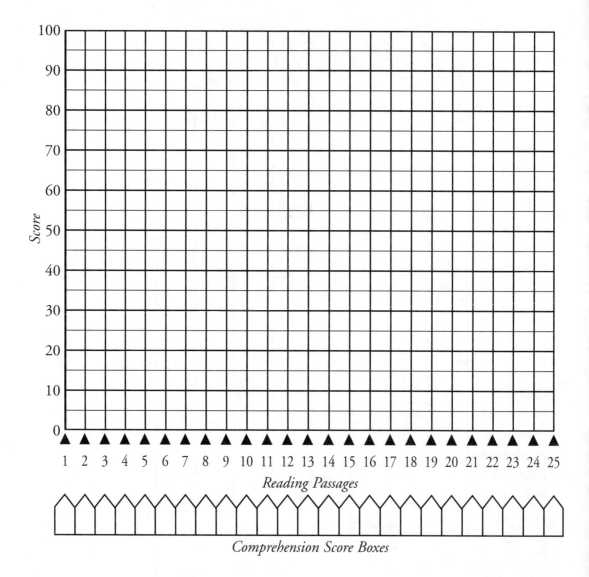

Reading Passages

Comprehension Score Boxes

Progress Graph: Passages 26–50

Directions: Write your Total Score for each passage in the comprehension score box under the number of the passage. Then plot your score on the graph itself by putting a small *x* on the line directly above the number of the passage, across from the score you got for that passage. As you mark your score for each passage, graph your progress by drawing a line to connect the *x*'s.

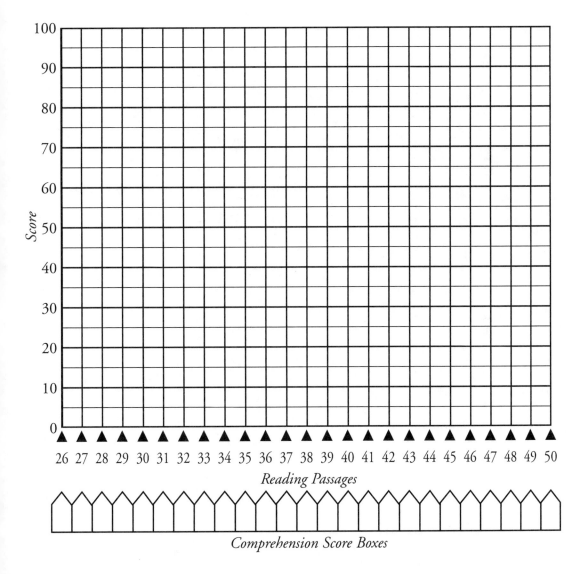

Reading Passages

Comprehension Score Boxes

Progress Graph: Passages 51–75

Directions: Write your Total Score for each passage in the comprehension score box under the number of the passage. Then plot your score on the graph itself by putting a small *x* on the line directly above the number of the passage, across from the score you got for that passage. As you mark your score for each passage, graph your progress by drawing a line to connect the *x*'s.

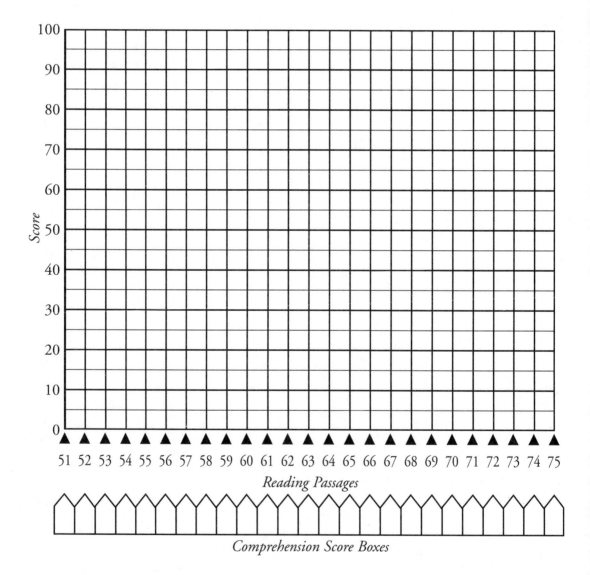

Reading Passages

Comprehension Score Boxes